TIGHT ROPE!

The Fun of Climbing

Dennis Gray leading *Namenlos* on Stanage, winter 1962/63.   Photo: D Whillans

TIGHT ROPE!

The Fun of
Climbing

Dennis Gray

 THE ERNEST PRESS

Published by The Ernest Press 1993
© Dennis Gray

ISBN 0 948153 25 3

British Library Cataloguing-in-Publication Data.
A Catalogue record for this book is available
from the British Library.

Typeset by EMS Phototypesetting, Berwick upon Tweed.
Printed by St. Edmundsbury Press.

Contents

Chapter One

Initiation

The Pack Horse in Woodhouse Lane, opposite Leeds University, has been the main meeting place for that institution's climbers for decades. Every Wednesday night in term time successive generations have met in the upstairs concert room to watch slide shows, discuss climbing and climbers and make arrangements for weekend meets. Whenever I am at home I try to attend, but every time I do and walk into that room, so typical of a Yorkshire pub, I am reminded of a more ancient group of drinkers who gathered there regularly during the last war; for it was up to that room I was occasionally taken as a young boy and listened whilst my father played the piano and entertained his Fire Brigade colleagues and other Service personnel. My dad had run away from home at nineteen years of age whilst a student at The Yorkshire College – a forerunner of the University – to try his luck on the stage in London. Although he never made it into the big time, he did earn a living as an entertainer for the rest of his life.

My sister and I grew up in a broken-down house of Yorkshire stone down the hill from the Pack Horse in the poor district of Woodhouse. Looking back now it seems that, although we were poor materially, our childhood was rich in happening and legend. It is difficult for me even now to distinguish between what my parents told me and what was reality. They were both expansive on occasion but at other times underplayed situations which, in other families, would have been the source of incredulity and scandal. My mother, being from a traditional Irish home, loved music and story and, though at times shaken by events, she remained until her early death what now would be dubbed a character. She was, I suppose, complementary to my father and his variety artist friends. She never protested too violently and remained totally loyal, even when my dad ended up in the debtors' prison for non-payment of taxes; or when one of his friends was arrested, during a visit to our house, for bigamy. The man in question, a tenor by the name of Jack Ramsay, was carted off to Armley jail, and my mother's comment was typical as she railed at the escorting police officers, "It's a bloody crime putting a man like that in a cold prison cell, it may damage his fine singing voice!"

1

She was possessed of a real temper, given free rein on occasion, whereupon her reactions were impressive for her diminutive figure. She had a friend in Leeds, another Irish lady, a certain Mrs Pape who was perhaps the most famous pub landlady of her time. One night, after a few gin and its, they started arguing about whether the licensee had the right to refuse entry to anyone she disliked. This led on to verbal abuse and then a full-scale fight, during which they threw at each other anything upon which they could lay their hands. It took many grown men to break up the resulting fracas, but amazingly the two women remained friends and had a good laugh when my father declared, in re-telling the story, that their battle had been more frightening than fighting the big fires from the Nazi bombing at Kirkstall Forge, when he had been hit and wounded by flying shrapnel.

My dad knew a lot of people in show business, took *The Stage* each week and played his engagements wearing formal apparel – usually evening dress, despite appearing most often in front of miners or other working men. He often boasted of being friendly with theatre people such as the Grade family, with whom he claimed to have shared shows and digs in his early stage career. I used to take these stories lightly until one night, when I had grown up, there was a knock on the door of my parents' house, and outside at the kerb was parked a Rolls Royce with a chauffeur at the wheel. It was one of the Grades – Leslie, I think – and he and my father greeted each other like long-lost brothers. The remainder of that evening was spent eating fish and chips out of a newspaper, drinking beer and telling stories. Eric Beard and I sat at their feet in my mother's kitchen whilst Leslie told joke after joke.

Because of my father's profession he did travel widely around the country in an old car, a Standard Ten with a beautiful oak-panelled dashboard, which eventually met its end one night whilst returning to Leeds from Scarborough. They hit a Wallace Arnold bus head-on in thick fog, and my mother attacked the poor, hapless bus driver with her handbag when he climbed down to enquire after their well-being. Such was my family environment when I started going out into the countryside in 1947. I met many unconventional characters and experienced adventures which in retrospect both surprise and frighten me, but at the time did not excite too much comment. I was then only eleven years old and, not knowing any better, guessed that the whole adult world was peopled by eccentrics who did crazy things – and I suppose that, beside wanting to learn to climb, I wanted to be like them and to gain their acceptance.

My first journeys out into the Yorkshire Dales were to Ingleton and to the Cow and Calf Rocks at Ilkley, the one set in beautiful limestone terrain, the other in a part-industrial, part-prehistoric landscape of millstone grit. It was on the latter I started to climb, and amid the former I did my first hill-walk (up Ingleborough) and descended my first cave. Both climbing and potholing were generally seen at that time as being something akin to Russian roulette, and definitely not for an eleven-year old. However, by sheer persistence over a period of two or three years, I managed to become part of the outdoor fraternity and an established member of an unusual group of climbers, mainly from Bradford and known as 'The Bradford Lads'. They were never a club and were held together solely by bonds of friendship and love of the sport. They were rich in diversity and, like many young people after the last war, were seeking adventure and a better life than their mainly working-class parents had been able to afford. What we did not realise at the time was that, without the social changes brought about by the war, our activities and subsequent journeys might not have been possible. The final years of the 1940s were to be the crucible of many changes which were to affect all of us: the setting up of the National Parks and improved access to the countryside; the introduction of the Health Service; and increasing opportunities in the educational field.

The young climbers of the group such as Marie Ball, Peter Greenwood, Harold and Neville Drasdo, Mike Dixon, Duncan Boston, Tom Ransley, Don Hopkin, Freddie Williams, Frank Cartwright, Bob Sowden and Alfie Beanland were bolstered by one or two older men who had been in the services, particularly Tom Cranfield and Syd Theakston: an unusual mixture of ages, ideas and generations, and almost without females. My earliest companions at Ilkley before I met the Bradford Lads were two climbers known as Cosher and Lazarus, plus George Elliot and his girlfriend, Luscious. Her proper name was Lushby, but we all knew her by her pseudonym, which aptly described her. The very first camp-follower I met, she would wait patiently for George whilst he climbed and snuggle up to him as soon as he returned to terra firma.

George was our star but his equipment was amazing. His sleeping bag was a large black overcoat in which he slept in barns and bivouacs, and into which he would pull Luscious before fastening it around them; and he climbed in either gym pumps or patent leather shoes which he had bought for a few pence at a jumble sale in Shipley. These latter made climbing harder, but for some reason he took great delight in solo-climbing routes like Gibbon's Wall at Ilkley while wearing them, and also his large, black overcoat, to give the impression to other climbers and tourists alike that he was just another sightseer. He was of medium height, in his early twenties

Some of the Bradford Lads in Langdale, 1952. L to R: John Ramsden (Ram), Doug Hayes, Duncan Boston, Mike Dawson, Bob Sowden, Jim Lyons, Marie Ball (Blake).   Photo: Gray coll.

and had a face best described as angular. He climbed very gymnastically and wore his gingery hair shoulder length, which in the 1940s was viewed as totally decadent. We concentrated on the Cow and Calf Rocks because they were easy to reach from Leeds and Bradford by the Samuel Ledgard's buses, and Ingleton because the Pennine Bus ran to that destination. None of our acquaintances owned their own transport and petrol was rationed. You simply travelled everywhere by bus or train, the latter infrequent at best in the post-war period of austerity.

Slowly, over the next few years, living standards improved for most of my companions, and we began to visit outcrops further afield but still in our own midden: crags set either on the fringe of beautiful moorland or in wooded valley scenery. These landscapes were peopled by those who lived mainly from the land, and their images have remained with me ever since: Almscliff Crag, Widdop, Earl Crag, Caley Crags, Rylstone and Crook Rise and the limestone country to the north known simply as The Dales. On my first visit to Crook Rise with, amongst others, Bob Sowden and Tom Cranfield, we found an unexploded bomb simply lying astride the footpath. I swore I could hear it ticking and ran off immediately in the opposite direction, for it seemed enormous to me, and I imagined being blown to pieces. But Tom, who had been in the para's and had fought at Arnhem, dressed as always in his jumping jacket and wearing his red beret, edged cautiously up to it and gave it a kick. Then it really did start ticking, and we ran all the way down to Skipton to report it to the police.

My earliest climbing equipment consisted of boots with triple hob-nails in their soles, a cut-down raincoat, a peaked cap from the mountain troops and a pair of pants made into breeches. We all wore white, ex-War Department ski socks

Tom Cranfield wearing his 'Para' beret and jacket, climbing in tricouni-nailed boots, Idwal, 1948.
Photo Gray coll.

and usually climbed in our nailed boots, tied onto natural fibre ropes that were adequate, at best for short leader falls, or at worst for seconds only. We rarely if ever top-roped any climb, and the prevailing attitude was that the leader should never fall. Peter Greenwood did on one occasion, whilst climbing on a hemp rope borrowed from Tom Cranfield. When his weight came onto his lifeline, it simply parted. As he lay on the ground, having fallen quite some distance, winded and nursing a sprained ankle, Tom appeared and gave him stick: "You stupid bugger, you've ruined me best rope. They're not for falling onto, you know, just for psychological purposes." Such was the accepted wisdom of the day!

My early caving experiences, which took place in the winter months, put me off the sport for the rest of my life. After several epics in potholes like Hell Hole near Grassington, I met my Waterloo at the age of fourteen down, of all places, the easy but sporting Attermire Cave above Settle. a party led by a slightly older boy, Peter Tuke, wearing flat caps with a candle stuck on the brim, we crawled and traversed our way, with an unavoidable swim through a sump, to the high chamber. We sat there, shivering but pleased with our efforts, until Peter, who was older and therefore knew more than we, insisted that we put out our candles before we used up all the oxygen and died of carbon monoxide poisoning. Candles extinguished, we found we could not see, of course, and tried to re-light them. After much panic Peter and the others got their candles to ignite, but mine refused however hard we tried. Getting back out of that cave without any light other than that provided by my friends in front proved to be a struggle; on one occasion I stepped straight out into space to land in a pool of ice-cold water up to my chest. The final straw was when we emerged from the cave to find it was snowing hard. Trying to get dry and changed, shivering in the mouth of the fissure, I got so cold that I was sure I had hypothermia as we staggered down the road to Settle to catch the bus home. I have never been caving since.

My second pair of boots had clinker nails. I bought them for a small sum from Luscious, she being confident by then that she would never really need them and preferring to watch us from the safety of level ground. I remember trying them out to lead the Very Difficult *Stewpot* at Almscliff and being immediately convinced that I would never be a VS man, an aspiration of every young climber in that era. I had not yet realised that nails were akin to roller skates on any climb which required a friction move, for you really need positive holds for nail climbing; and as I stood up on the sloping shelf of the crux, fifteen feet from the ground, my heart was in my mouth. It was a long while before I dared to try anything harder. Tom Cranfield had made it plain to us all that gym pumps were only to be used on hard climbs, and that if you used them on easy routes you were a climbing cissy.

Over the next two years and by about the summer of 1950, the release of WD equipment made from new materials developed for the war effort began to have its effect on the sport. Ski boots with vibram soles, known to us as Commandos, began to appear. They were, in retrospect, useless compared to later custom-built climbing boots, but we marvelled at their construction and thought them great for climbing despite their square toes. I could not get a suitable pair because they were all in large foot sizes, but Peter Greenwood was determined, despite facing the same problem, to get a pair. The fact that he had to wear seven pairs of socks to make them fit was not a barrier to him, and when I recall that he used to climb in them up and down The Spider Wall, a difficult problem for that era, I wonder whether we do not now place too much emphasis on equipment and too little on the skill of the climber?

Nylon ropes began to appear, and the first ones I remember, being tow-ropes which had been used to pull gliders were not, of course, of the right tensile strength for climbing. There were some nasty accidents before climbers learned how to use nylon ropes properly but, once this had been accomplished, the extra security they gave over natural fibre ropes was partly responsible for the great leap forward in climbing standards in the 1950s.

Businesses were established at that time selling nothing but ex-WD equipment – everything from a generator to an ice-axe. I bought my first axe from a mail-order firm in Manchester for what is now fifteen pence. It is interesting that a decade later Robin Smith used exactly the same model, specially shortened for steep ice-climbing, for all his great winter climbs in Scotland. I still possess his axe, retrieved from a snowdrift at the foot of Ben Nevis's Gardyloo Buttress from where he had dropped it. Snap-links (karabiners) became available from such shops and, although nobody knew their history or reliability, we found we were better off with them. It was a while before slings of various thickness became available to use as running belays on climbs and, initially, we used snap-links only to belay with, leading most of our climbs totally without protection. There were equipment innovators in our ranks, however, and many experiments were made around this time at Ilkley; some have passed into local climbing folklore.

Dave Gibbons, a regular at the outcrop, was known as 'Chiphole' for his technique of cutting holds in the rock-face to create climbs, local testpieces such as the Cow's Udder and his eponymous wall in the Quarry. These activities were frowned upon by many traditionalists, but Dave cared little for their opinion, seeing himself as the Van Gogh of the climbing world. Fortunately, this bastard practice did cease for a while once he had emigrated, like many other young climbers of that era, to Australia. Before this he developed a climbing machine similar to a bicycle that you pedalled up the rock-face. However, you had to have a rope fixed from above and it was difficult to achieve progress on overhanging rock.

Arthur Dolphin, one of my mentors, was then the area's leading climber; he used to carry out experiments to test ropes with a karabiner of his own design. It had a gate and a friction groove into which the rope slid once it had reached a certain loading. However, this was abandoned after one of the rope holders burnt his hands quite badly, for not everyone realised, when nylon ropes first appeared, their potential for burning human flesh!

At about this time we began to meet every Sunday night in a café in Otley, 'Tommies', a place of inimitable decor and furnished as were the soup-kitchens of old. For the next few years 'Tommies' was an essential gathering place at the end of each weekend's climbing, when climbing news was exchanged and future meets arranged. Otley was chosen because it was equidistant from Leeds and Bradford, but also because of its position as the true gateway to the Yorkshire Dales. It held close associations for me as my father's birthplace; some of my relations were still living there. In 'Tommies' we got to know many other outdoor enthusiasts: cavers, ramblers and cyclists, the leading light amongst whom was a tall, thin, sinewy blond guy with a flat Leeds accent, called Jimmy Savile, who kept everybody amused with his biking tales. He started his meteoric career as – I'm not sure quite how to describe him; I suppose you would now say a disc jockey, but they had not then been invented – organising Sunday night dances for the outdoor fraternity, before moving on to the Leeds Mecca and stardom. He and the late Eric Beard were almost doppelgangers, both from the same area of Leeds 6; and it is an interesting conjecture that if Eric, who became one of the greatest fell-runners of all time, had survived the car crash which killed him in 1969, he might also have been Knighted, for he, too, was an entertainer of talent.

It was around 1950 that some of my older companions decided to visit the Continent, despite the fact that the Alps then seemed as remote as the Himalaya. The journey was totally beyond my means as a schoolboy, but I followed their plans and discussions with as keen an interest as if I had been a member of the proposed team. At that time knowledge of how to go about such an undertaking was limited, and after discussing the pros and cons at great length one night in Otley, it was decided that Alfie Beanland would renew contact with an old and senior warrior whom we had met occasionally at Ilkley and who had been an Alpinist before the war. Alfie was to find out from him how to go about making all the arrangements for such an expedition. A few weeks later, at another of our Sunday night get-togethers, a totally bemused Alfie reported back to his eager fellow Alpine novices: "It appears there are only three cardinal rules to Alpinism, and if they are strictly followed any fool can climb the classic routes!" – "What are they?" gasped his eager audience and Alfie, who was a great man for the melodramatic, held them in suspense for a moment before reporting the old mountaineer's advice: "Firstly, always book through Thomas Cook's, secondly, follow the guides because they know the way and, finally, always keep your ice-axe in front of you!" At this piece of sagacity, his audience almost fell off their chairs laughing.

Petrol rationing finished in the spring of 1950 and from garages, barns and outhouses the length of the land appeared ancient vehicles and motor bikes, the names of which now read like a roll-call of the dead; since that date the demise of these famous names of British motoring has been almost

Alfie Beanland taking an afternoon bathe in the Llanberis Pass, 1952.   Photo: T Ransley

total – Austin, Brough Superior, Scott, Alvis, Standard, Jowett, Rudge, Ariel, Panther, Royal Enfield, Douglas, Wolseley and so many more. But in 1950 they were polished up and their mainly middle-class owners started to drive freely again. We made the major discovery that we could cadge lifts, and thus roam much farther afield. The Lake District became our favourite area and Wall End Barn and the Langdale Valley our mecca. Hitch-hiking is almost an art form and there are a lot of tactics to learn if one is to be successful. We learned the hard way and it took me a long time before I mastered all the finer points of the technique – I found at night that you had almost to walk out and under the front bumper of some cars to make sure the driver had seen you. My greatest asset was my youth and I am ashamed to report that I used to spin such hard luck stories to drivers that on occasion I actually made a profit on weekend trips to Langdale. Drivers would press upon me monetary gifts to help me in my terrible plight, stuck as I was without food or money (which was true), and not knowing when I might, if ever, see my parents again.

There were, however, few cars on the road despite the derationing of petrol. Often one faced the mental torture of arriving at the start of the A65 just outside Kendal – the hitch-hiker's graveyard – to find ten or twelve

The hitch-hiker's art: Phil Gordon in action, 1950s.   Photo: D Stone

Peter Greenwood leading *Traditional Climb*, Almscliff, 1949.   Photo: Greenwood coll.

Wall End Barn, Great Langdale. One of the spiritual homes of climbers in the late 40s and 50s.   Photo: C Murdoch.

other Yorkshire climbers lined up, trying to persuade a car to stop and take them southwards. It then required ingenuity and determination to keep your pole position at the end of the queue, for to be last was to be first and the Lads would try many stunts to get behind you in the queue – everything from crawling behind hedges through the muddy fields, dodging into shop or house doorways, or hiding up a tree, as happened on one occasion whilst I walked past. I do recall that Freddie Williams' trick one Sunday was to sit on the kerb with a leg swathed in bandages, declaring he could not walk down the road as he had suffered a terrible accident the day before, climbing in Easedale. Feeling sorry for him, we allowed him to stay put and moved on, only for him to pass us a short while later reclining in the back of a large limousine, from which he waved a rude V sign at us. When we arrived at Tommies later that night, much later, after a miserable number of hours reaching our destination via an interminable number of lifts, there was Freddie hunched over a pint of tea with no sign of the bandages, but sporting a grin which said it all.

For almost two years we hitch-hiked everywhere, and by this method I travelled to Skye, Glencoe, North Wales and many times to the Lake District. I had two marvellous lifts which I will always remember: one in an Aston Martin with Whitehead, the world rally car champion (he was killed a few weeks later in the Tulip Rally); and one with Smith, the world motor-cycle trials champion, on a factory-prepared BSA. This last gave me the ride of a lifetime – just like being in the TT!

During this period we stayed in barns, sleeping, initially, in blankets. We became experts at finding barns which offered the possibility of a night's uninterrupted kip, hidden from potentially irate farmers, lying buried in the straw. We also stayed in youth hostels, our membership of which was solely for the purpose of utilising their facilities to enable us to get out climbing. We only did this for a short period, for The Bradford Lads and youth hostel wardens were an explosive mixture. In retrospect I have to concede that the fault did lie in our youthful exuberance, but in those days most of the gentlemen who ran these establishments (they were at that time almost exclusively male) appeared to have been recruited from retired members of the military or, to judge by their demeanour, perhaps even from the German SS.

Our first run-in with a warden was at Elterwater after coming off Raven Crag, Walthwaite, on a dark winter's evening. We were still wearing all our warm clothes and the warden insisted we remove our woollen Jaeger balaclavas as a mark of respect as we signed in. Peter Greenwood refused to

L to R: Dennis Gray, Peter Greenwood and Frank Cartwright (Chuck Chuck) at Almscliff,
1952.
                                                                        Photo: T Ransley

comply, for the man's language was abusive; at this, in a rage, the guy leaned
over and pulled the offending hat off its owner's head. This was too much
for Peter who, although only seventeen, hit him. A free-for-all ensued with a
wrestling match which would have done credit to Big Daddy and co., but
which ended with our being kicked out to hitch and walk our way for most of
what was left of the night to the Wall End Barn.

A similar incident occurred when Jim Lyons, Duncan Boston and I had climbed late on Scafell and arrived at eleven o'clock at night at the door of the Longthwaite Youth Hostel in Borrowdale, only to find it shuttered and closed and apparently no one in residence. None of us wished to spend the night out in the open without a sleeping bag, so I, being young and innocent, was pushed forward to rap on the warden's door. I knocked louder and louder. Eventually a light came on, and the Obengruppenführer arrived, framed in its portal.

"What do you want?" he growled.

"To stay in the hostel. We are all members," I stammered.

"At this time of night! Don't you know what hour it is?"

I tried to placate him with a hard luck story about being stuck on Jones' Direct Route on the Pinnacle Face of Scafell (which was in fact true), claiming that having lost my watch (which at that date I could not afford to possess), I had not known the time.

"Watch! Watch!" he screamed, almost beside himself with rage. "You don't need a watch, laddie. At this time of night, you need a calendar!" and he slammed the door in our faces, condemning us to spend a cold and cheerless night in a barn in Langstrath.

After many such experiences at youth hostels our final contretemps occurred at Ambleside Youth Hostel, on the site of what is now the Queen's Hotel. We would aim to reach there on a Friday night, hitch-hiking up from Leeds or Bradford (via Skipton, Ingleton, Kendal and Windermere), rising early on Saturday morning for the first bus trip up to Langdale, Keswick or Coniston. If one of our number could get inside before the hostel's doors closed for the evening, he would then make sure that any other climbers arriving later could get in by surreptitiously opening the bolted front door or a window in the self-cookers' kitchen. This scam held until early one Saturday morning when, with only one of our number officially booked into the hostel, the warden by chance looked into his self-cooking kitchen and could not believe his eyes at the number of climbers bent over gas-rings, stirring porridge pans and frying bacon. The resulting tirade of abuse on both sides finished my own short experience of youth hostelling for, with their inevitably rigid rule-orientated method of administration, they could not then provide for our needs. Despite the fact that they were at times a battleground caused by different expectations, my hostelling days were a rich experience.

At about this time I became a 'Wanted Boy'. One winter Sunday morning of abysmal weather, Frank 'Chuck Chuck' Cartwright and myself left Langdale to hitch-hike home. We always dreaded wet weather for not many car drivers would pick you up once you were dripping, too wary of damaging their upholstery. This occasion was no exception and we were on the road for almost 48 hours, arriving home via a lift in a meat lorry full of carcasses. My father waited until the Monday night and, when I did not arrive home, called the police. Once initiated, it took a few days to call off the subsequent missing boy hunt, for communications in 1951 were not what they are now, and all my known places of visit were searched. Climbers staying in Wall End Barn, drinkers in the Dungeon Ghyll Bar, hostellers, walkers, car drivers were all questioned, and though this reaction might seem a bit extreme viewed from today's perspective, it is a fact that only a few weeks earlier two girls had got lost between Grasmere and Elterwater and, despite their being on a minor road, had died in a blizzard. I myself had been out helping to look for them. Unfortunately, the police had not told anyone why they were looking for me, only enquiring, "Does anyone know this youth?" Thus, when I next arrived in the Lake District, it was almost as if I had been one of the Great Train Robbers, and several people contacted the police, informing them of my whereabouts, much to their and my annoyance.

This event had its sequel, though, for Chuck Chuck bought a motor-bike, as did many others of our number who had recently experienced similar difficulties whilst hitch-hiking. Inevitably, as numbers on the road grew ever larger and tolerance from car owners waned, it became more and more difficult to obtain lifts. But the country had begun to recover from the War and standards of living were rising as more people were able to purchase consumer products – motor-bikes and cars. The great egalitarian march was under way, at last.

It was seeing Arthur Dolphin climb at Ilkley on my first visit to the Quarry in 1947 which made me want to climb. So when later I was able to climb with him, travel on his motor-bike and visit his home in Leeds – as a friend, despite my extreme youth – I knew I was fortunate to know such a person. Beside his climbing prowess, he was a keen athlete, running cross-country for Yorkshire, a caver and an enthusiastic motor-cyclist. He was a metallurgist, from a different social background than most of The Bradford Lads, and had graduated from Leeds University. He looked like a wraith, tall and gangling, with white hair and an albino complexion. His story is well known to many climbers, for his great pioneering climbs in the Lake District, such as Hell's Groove on Scafell (with Peter Greenwood) and Deer Bield Buttress, and his tragic death in the Alps in 1953 are well-documented. However, my own favourite anecdotes about him have never before appeared in print, to the best of my knowledge.

Arthur Dolphin leading the first ascent of *Baskerville*, Raven Crag, Langdale, 1949.
Photo: Gray coll.

In 1952 he purchased one of the new 350cd BSA Gold Star motor-bikes, supposed to be the first production model of that capacity able to 'do the ton'. One Wednesday night after taking me out climbing at Ilkley, he decided that, having run the machine in, he would test it for the manufacturer's claims. With me on the pillion, heading down Hollin's Hill towards Shipley, he gave it full throttle but, despite our crouching low, he could not get it over 90mph. He contacted the dealer from whom he had purchased the machine. There was little sympathy from this quarter and, after some minor tinkering, his complaint was more or less ignored. Much to Arthur's disgust, once out on the roads again, these adjustments still left the Gold Star with a top speed well below the magic 'ton'.

The next time I went round to his house in Old Farnley, Leeds, the engine and the gearbox were laid out on newspapers around the living-room floor: thousands of pieces in a bewildering mass of metal – at least, so it appeared to me. But a few weeks later, after he had put it all back together, we tried again down the Otley Chevin on our way to an evening's bouldering at Caley Crags. This time, to his great satisfaction, we notched up 103mph, which felt incredible to me at that time, bobbing up and down behind him on the back of the bike. "It was a small problem with the transmission ... that's all!" he modestly informed me as we walked up to the crag.

Another memory of him comes from the winter of 1952 when we visited Malham, where he and I stayed at some kind of hut which was used mainly by cavers. Earlier that day Arthur had taken me up the frozen waterfall in Gordale to teach me the technique of ice-climbing, and afterwards we had been looking around for rock-climbing possibilities at The Cove. He was very well known in the potholing world, for in those days many enthusiasts were active in both sports and he was as famous for his exploits underground as on the rock-face. (The cavers were an even more boisterous crowd than the climbers in that period and certainly drank a lot more beer. A feature of the epoch was the sing-songs, and we in the Bradford Lads had our own original numbers such as *The Calypso* (which was then all the rage), the *Juvenile Delinquent*, which was later attributed wrongly to Tom Patey, and *In Langdale's Green Valley*; the words of some of these would have made a rugby team blush). We spent the Saturday evening in the pub, and the cavers almost lifted the rafters with their singing; and, although Arthur neither drank alcohol nor smoked nor sang, he seemed to enjoy their company very much. Once back in the hut, a games session was organised. Many of these were traditional amongst climbers and cavers – Indian and Chinese wrestling, putting out the beer bottles, placing the match stick. Arthur loved

Billy Maxwell diving over chairs at the Sandstone dinner, High Rocks Inn, 1959.
Photo: A Mayes

these contests and was as keen as anybody I ever saw. He actually practised some of them at home mid-week, as he felt they were good for keeping you in trim for rock-climbing.

The evening ended with the cavers organising a fingertip pull-up competition, using on a small ledge set above the door-frame of the hut and with a bottle of whisky as a prize, which in those days was really something. I managed about three, the best of the cavers seven or eight, but Arthur, making his bid last, achieved seventeen. "You must develop your finger strength if you want to climb hard!" he often advised me, and there is no doubt he had done just that. I will never forget just how good he was both as a person and a climber. Some of his boulder problems at Almscliff such as the *Teaspoon Variation* – which I once saw him climb in his motor-cycle gear – still defeat some of the Lycra-clad, sticky-shoed rock-athletes of today. He declined the prize of the bottle of whisky, which was emptied that night by the rest of the company in the form of 'Mummery's Blood'. This should really be made with rum and Bovril, but to keep the cold at bay on that freezing night it was made with malt.

The potholers could be even more outrageous on occasion than ourselves, and one of their number, Duggie Bell, was a surprise to us all. He was youthfully good-looking, always spotlessly clean, quiet-spoken, well-

Ye Olde Naked Man Café, Settle, where the 'BSA' (the pot-holers) hung out in the late 40s and
50s.   Photo: W Todd

mannered and smartly dressed and so, when he misbehaved, it took
everybody by surprise, especially those who had not made his acquaintance.
The cavers' headquarters in those days was the old British Speological
Association hut (known to us all as the BSA) in Settle, and some of the inn-
keepers, café and chip-shop owners in that town had serious reservations
about their presence, due to their occasional wild activities. One chip-shop
banned them after one such incident and so Duggie decided to retaliate. His
opportunity came one day when an unfortunate cat was run over and killed
near the hut. Duggie, in his usual good-mannered, apparently helpful way,
offered to give the poor tabby a decent burial, in order to relieve its grieving
owner of this sad task. However, he used the cadaver later that night, when
the chip-shop was full of customers, to get his revenge. He marched in and
lobbed the corpse over the counter and straight into the number one vat,
which was seething with boiling chip-oil. "There, fry that you nasty
buggers!" were his immortal words as he about-turned and marched out,
leaving behind an astounded audience and an even more paralysed fish fryer
as witness to the cremation.

Jack Bradley joined our ranks in Langdale on his return from Australia.

He and several other climbers and cavers had been out there on government-assisted passage schemes. For a small sum you could go to Australia or Canada but, once there, you had to stay at least two years. The intent was that you would go there and not come back, for it was a good way of slimming down the dole queues, which were once again lengthening as in the depression years of the 1930s. Jack's group had used this scheme mainly as a way of travelling around and climbing before returning home once more. My first meeting with him was whilst hitch-hiking on the road to Skipton, when he was dressed in a duffle coat. This was then his only real outdoor equipment and, like George Elliot's overcoat, was used on occasion as a sleeping bag in barns and, on others, as an awkward climbing jacket – he had returned from Australia almost destitute, and I remember him telling us that he had only £3 in the whole world! Within months, however, he had founded the beginnings of his building empire, and only a short while later some of my Langdale climbing friends were working for him on a site in Yorkshire, constructing houses in the boom years of the early 1950s. He paid them mainly in beer and after work they simply continued the roistering, hard-living life to which they had become accustomed at weekends. But Jack was no dilettante; within three or four years his house-building had made him a millionaire, and within a few more years a multi-millionaire, at which point he wisely retired.

Before his rise to riches, Jack had become a legend in our Bradford Lads' sagas with *The Brass Bound Buggery Box*. This was a Triumph 650cc, purchased with some of the first earnings from his business and onto which he had fitted a side-car racing frame; on this he had then built, to his own design, a large, black box, with brass staves holding it together. On occasion, five of us rode on this contraption at incredible speeds up and down Langdale after pub closing time. It met its end in a dramatic crash at the bends of the Whoop Hall Pub on the road between Kendal and Ingleton. In those days the A65 road between Skipton and Kendal was a sporting motor-cyclist's dream, with its steeply banked and sharp corners, only very short straights and right-angled bridges at Ingleton and Cowan Bridge. To average a mile a minute, you had to be a master at handling your machine. Probably it would not now be possible to ride in such fashion anywhere on the open roads in the UK, and certainly the A65 is changed out of all recognition, for even the Whoop Hall bends have been bypassed.

In 1952, however, things were different and one Sunday night, driving home late after a weekend's climbing, Jack was at the controls of the Box with his faithful side-car partner, Chuck Chuck, alongside him in full racing leathers, throwing himself all over the machine to keep the frame down on terra firma. Unfortunately, out of the goodness of his heart, Jack had picked up three of The Lads sooner than leave them behind hitching on the road. Thus, from Kendal southwards, he was forced into driving his contraption with three bodies hanging onto the Box, for, other than Chuck Chuck, two were total novices at the art of leaning, with, in addition, Harold Drasdo on the pillion seat. Going into the Whoop Hall bends the command came from the driver, "Lean!" but he forgot to tell them which way. Chuck Chuck got it right, – but the other two, one of whom was the infamous Pale Man, who later ended up in jail for stealing a Triumph Twin motor-cycle, both leaned in the opposite direction. This was enough to upset their equilibrium and as Jack was changing down, screaming through the gears at about 60mph, it upset his line and the Buggery Box's adhesion; the frame rose up like a thing possessed, causing the bike and its passengers to somersault and then cartwheel down the road, like a member of the Red Army ensemble.

Later, in Tommies, Harold Drasdo held us enthralled as he retold the story of how the bodies were distributed along the road as the bike careered along. Amazingly, no one was badly injured, though initially there were fears for the Pale Man, who was lying unconscious on the tarmac in a pool of blood. Harold, who had simply leapt off the pillion and stopped dead, almost as if dismounting a horse, had rushed up and, cradling the Pale Man's head in his arms, was saying the magic words, "Speak to me Pale Man, for God's sake, speak to me ..... someone fetch an ambulance." At these words Jack Bradley, who had been picking himself up and dusting himself down, came rushing into their act. "For Christ's sake, no, the Buggery Box is not insured to carry three passengers!" Fortunately, the Pale Man was revived by a passing motorist with a brandy flask who enquired, after surveying the wreckage, "What on earth were you all doing riding in a Bond mini car?" at which the Pale Man struggled to his feet and, though cut and bleeding, managed a rueful, "Hitching a lift!" as the confused motorist drove off, shaking his head.

Barns situated in the climbing areas of Great Britain became, in the early 1950s, places of unusual pilgrimage for the sport's mainly youthful and impecunious activists, few of whom were members of the old established climbing clubs. Any weekend in the summer of 1951, at Wall End in Great Langdale, Gatesgarth in Buttermere, Williams' in Idwal or Cameron's Barn in Glencoe you would have found a horde of young people sleeping rough, dressed mainly in ex-WD clothes and behaving on occasion in a wild and irresponsible fashion. I read somewhere that there have never been many fights amongst the climbing fraternity, just a lot of posturing and jockeying for position. This was not my experience as a small boy when I was a regular at Wall End Barn and I witnessed several slugging matches that would have done credit to Frank Tyson or Cassius Clay. I myself was never involved, being a coward, a wee boy and in any case a pacifist by nature and belief. But I well remember, amongst other contests, Peter Greenwood battling it out with another climber known to us as Pablo, in a fight which finished only when Peter, who was outclassed, outweighed and out-aged, was knocked senseless; and Death Whitwell versus The Agnew, which was more in the nature of a wrestling match, as both climbers were good amateurs at the sport; this one ended up for real with bodies being flung around the barn. No one could remember afterwards what the fights had been about, and usually the pugilists were soon the best of friends again. I suppose it was very much a working class way of settling disputes at that date; it was a case of no sooner a word than an apology or a blow!

Peter Greenwood, five years older than me, was our wild man but one of the most generous and kind persons I have known. However, his philosophy of life was to give way to no man either on the road or in the barns and, once set out, you completed your climb whatever the conditions. That he has survived into old age seems a miracle to me, and if a cat has nine lives, he must have ten. His motor-cycling record of spills puts him at the top of 'fender benders', but his falls whilst climbing were equally impressive. I do not want to give a false impression of his abilities; he was a brilliant rock-climber, one of the very best of my generation – for instance, it was he who, at the first attempt, solved the difficult sequence of moves that gained entrance into *Hell's Groove*, which climb he pioneered with Arthur Dolphin. However, it is hard for the young climbers from today's affluent society to understand what it was like – how much time and effort the carless and impecunious climbers of the 1950s had to invest to reach their destination in order to climb. If you were as gifted a climber as Peter you became angry and impatient and often, in order to achieve his ambitions, he would attempt climbs in terrible conditions, leading with socks over the basketball boots in which he often climbed.

He had many spectacular escapes, in particular whilst climbing Deer Bield Buttress in a rainstorm, when he fell off the final pitch and pulled his second man, Freddie Williams, from his stance (they finished the climb); and the big fall he had off Scafell's Central Buttress in the wet; but, for me, his most amazing fall was off a more humble cliff, namely the Eastern Buttress of Raven Crag in Langdale. He had led a climb called *Nineveh* in winter with snow thick on the ground. Climbing confidently despite the conditions, he had led this quickly in a single run-out of over eighty feet but, on reaching the top of the crag, found himself in deep, treacherous snow. Kicking steps in his gym pumps and pulling up on heather, he was battling his way up this and had nearly reached a safe stance when, to the horror of those watching from below, the heather gave way and the slope avalanched, taking him with it. He calmly sized up the position and turned the fall into a jump, trying to pick out a good landing; with a giant leap he landed in the snow at the base of the cliff. Those watching expected to see a corpse at the end of this tremendous ride through space, but they were confounded when Peter slowly stood up in triumph, trying to brush off the snow with a single hand. But even he could not escape totally unhurt from such a tumble and, though he tried to hide it, his other arm hung useless by his side, for it was fractured. It was, nevertheless, a miraculous performance which few others would have survived, for his coolness in a potentially fatal situation had saved his life.

Chapter Two

Seduction in Langdale

The barns and other climbing dosses were, I suppose, an unusual type of finishing school for youngsters like myself. From my older companions I learned about trends in music, literature and art, discussed politics and religion and heard a lot about sex. At that time, from what I observed, there was an awful lot of talking about the subject, but not much action. Wall End Barn was not a brothel, whatever the locals might have thought about it, although the few young couples who inhabited the place did, on occasion, indulge in what is now termed 'love-making'; but never as some kind of public spectacle – it was always after the last candle was out. I did, on occasion, as a fourteen-year-old, lie with imagination running riot, keenly listening for heavy breathing, something I had learnt about from my older companions. On a couple of occasions, when hitch-hiking, I was pro-positioned by homosexuals, but they left me alone once I had made it plain that the attraction was not mutual! My first experience of real 'climbing' sex was as a voyeur, whilst staying in the Road Menders' Hut, which used to be situated under The Cromlech Boulders in Llanberis. This was a small, wooden shack with a tin roof which had been built especially for the road menders to shelter from the rain (frequent in the Llanberis Pass), but which the climbing fraternity quickly made their own.

The Rock and Ice had used the place from the club's earliest beginnings in 1951, even though it was against the law. On at least one occasion one of their number, Tom Waghorn, had been arrested and carted off to the Police Station with the intention of discouraging further use. We, nevertheless, continued to stay there, risking incarceration sooner than brave the elements outside, for none of us possessed nor could afford a tent. The hut was only of tiny dimensions but as many as a dozen of us would crowd in there, snuggling together like the proverbial bugs in a rug.

However, on the occasion I am now reporting there were only three of us in residence, one mid-week evening in the summer of 1952. I was on school holidays and my companions were unemployed; they were two members of the Creag Dhu Club from Glasgow, The Miller and Mick Noon. The latter and I had become good friends from a chance meeting in Idwal and we had subsequently climbed together on The Cobbler and in the Pass. Earlier that

The Road-mender's Hut in Llanberis, 1951. Pat Walsh is sat on the step nearest the *Cromlech Boulder* and Ginger Cain is stood on the right.   Photo: C Vigano

year I had visited Mick's home in the Gorbals' Denmark Street. It had made a tremendous impression on me, Leeds 6 being a rose garden in comparison: it was an endless ocean of run-down tenements but peopled with some of the kindest folk I had yet met, whose cheerfulness and sense of humour transcended their terrible environment. Mick was an outstanding example of this triumph over mind-numbing conditions.

On the night in question it was terrible weather with the rain drumming hard on the tin roof, and we had retired into our blankets and sleeping bags when we heard a car pull up at the door of the hut. It manoeuvred its way off the road until it was almost touching the step of the refuge. "It's the polis!" I heard the others whisper, as we lay there in the darkness with hearts pounding, expecting the law to push at any moment against the big rock we had wedged on the inside of the door to impede their entry. I could hear my companions' quick breathing and felt my own heart racing. "When will they put us out of our misery?" A quarter of an hour passed and, apart from rustling by the door, nothing happened. Eventually Mick, the oldest, crept forward and, peering through a crack in the fabric of the door, looked out from the darkness of the hut into the fading light of a wet summer's evening. We heard his chuckle and then the whispered command, "Come here and take a load o' this, boys!" The Miller and I crept forward and took it in turns to peep out through another crack adjacent to the one being monopolised by Noon.

Across the seat of the car, legs through the window, a couple was engaged in vigorous coupling, going at it without a care in the world. I watched, fascinated, and I felt an arousal of my own. "Git oot o' it, yer dirty hounds!" Mick suddenly shouted with a loud scream, just as I had taken over from the Miller for a third viewing. The couple in the car almost turned themselves into contortionists, trying to right themselves and replace unfastened clothes, but eventually they managed and, without waiting to find out who was in the hut, the driver revved the engine, reversed the car and drove off up the Pass as if the hounds of hell were at their heels. We collapsed in a heap, laughing, and during our climbing over the next few days we would repeat the mantra, "Git oot o' it, yer dirty hounds!"

Later that same week I sat alone on a wall at the side of the Pass road, not far from the entrance to Ynys Ettws, the Climbers' Club hut, watching my friends climb on the cliff of Carreg Wasted above. A middle-aged, greying, curly-haired man of powerful physique and medium height wandered up the road and on reaching my perch, sat down, without a word, on the wall close to me. I guessed he was a climber by his dress, but we both sat there for some considerable time in complete silence. The situation was beginning to unnerve me when, suddenly, the figure at my side turned and said to me in quite an angry tone of voice, "Are you one of those young socialists from West Kirby?". This completely stunned me, and hesitatingly I answered, pointing up Carreg Wasted to two figures high on Shadow Wall, "Er....no. I'm with those two lads up there from Glasgow. They're members of the Creag Dhu," hoping this would impress him and stop him asking any more such questions. "You're a socialist, aren't you? Don't tell me lies. Everybody tells me lies!" I began to get frightened now, for his voice was becoming increasingly angry and I had no idea then that this person was mentally ill. "I'm a climber, I'm a schoolboy!" I stuttered, expecting at any minute to be attacked. But suddenly he calmed down and smiled at me. "That's alright then. Would you like to do a climb?" he demanded. "With you? But I'm with those two older boys up there," I stalled. "Are they your brothers?" "Yes!" I lied, trying to fake a Glaswegian accent. The stranger began to mutter to himself and then, suddenly pointing upwards, said, "That climb they are on

– I think I made the first ascent of that?" Incredulous, I said rather pompously, "Oh no, that was pioneered by the great John Menlove Edwards. It's Shadow Wall." (In passing it is worth noting that in 1952 this route was still considered a serious and hard climb.) My companion did not appear to hear this but began muttering to himself once more, which worried me even further. Suddenly he stood up and, apparently regaining control, smiled at me and, looking straight into my eyes, declared, "I'm Edwards!" I was stunned. Here was one of my greatest heroes, but not as I had expected him, for the stories then current in the climbing world were from an earlier epoch, from the man's youth. He was supposed to be a phenomenon, a man of immense strength, but there were also dark hints that he was a homosexual. He put his hand lightly on my left shoulder, laughed – a laugh whose sound will stay with me always, for it contained a note of desperation – and said simply, "Good luck! enjoy your climbing." He tightened his grip for a brief second and I felt something akin to an electric shock shoot down my side. He let go and ambled off back up the road towards the entrance to Ynys. He looked a little pathetic, nothing like I expected my heroes to look, and I never saw him again.

Several years later, after Edwards' tragic suicide but long before the present trend for his elevation into the pantheon of climbing saints, I contacted his sister, the painter Nowell Johnson. My interest in his prose writings, his poetry and his investigations and theories of psychiatry had aroused my deep curiosity about the man and his works. Thus, twenty years ago, I journeyed to Canterbury to visit his sister, who was married to the 'Red' Dean, Hewlett Johnson, at the Deanery. Unfortunately, when it was bombed during the last war, some of Edwards' papers were lost, and subsequently most of his writings on his psychiatric work were destroyed. I read all the remaining works, poems and writing, and this was enough to convince me that the man was a unique, brilliant but tragic person. I was truly happy when recently Jim Perrin wrote a first-class record and interpretation of his life in his award winning book, *Menlove*.

My second experience of 'climbing' sex was to be in the first person. In the late summer of 1952, still only sixteen years of age, I had started to study and work in the printing industry and had to report to the works in Leeds on Saturday mornings in case there were any errands to be run and urgent mail to be dealt with. This meant, of course, that my weekends were curtailed, but if I was lucky I was away by 10 am, and if I was even more fortunate with good lifts, I could reach the Lake District by late afternoon, still in time for a climb. This is exactly what had occurred one fine Saturday of excellent

Some Bradford Lads outside the Old Dungeon Ghyll, 1952. Jack Bradley is on the motor-bike and Peter Greenwood is stood next to him.   Photo: Greenwood coll.

weather at the end of September as I strode into the bar of the Old Dungeon Ghyll Hotel, rucksack on my back, looking for someone with whom to do a route. Disappointment greeted me for none of my friends was there. The only person present was a small, dark, attractive woman who, I found out later, was thirty years of age. I was about to go back out into the bright, sunlit afternoon, when she suddenly rose to her feet, "Are you little Dennis?" she smilingly enquired. "Er...yes?" I replied without much enthusiasm. "Oh, good, your friends told me you would take me climbing!" I was embarrassed by this piece of news and stood by the door awaiting further developments. She came over and held out her hand, "I'm X. I'm an artist, but I am also a climber. Do you think you could lead me up *Bilberry Buttress*? I've always wanted to climb that route!" I swallowed hard; I had never climbed *Bilberry Buttress* on Raven Crag on the hillside above the hotel, for it had quite a reputation in that era for difficulty. I knew it consisted of a succession of difficult cracks and was over 200 feet high, but by that date I had led routes of comparable standard. "I'll try!" I decided, and after I had stowed my rucksack behind the bar, and she had gone off to change in the hotel, returning in breeches and a sweater, we set out.

Bilberry Buttress lies on the right-hand side of the main buttress of Raven Crag and starts at the foot of a small ridge leading up to a steep crack. We soon reached and located the foot of our climb and roped up. Just as I was about to set forth, the lady grabbed and embraced me. "Good luck!" she whispered in my ear, and then planted a kiss on my cheek – not a motherly peck but a full, passionate, heavy-breathing job that made me break away and scamper up that first ridge in absolute terror. "Maybe I was mistaken?" I wondered, as I looked around for a belay, for I was totally inexperienced in these matters. Once I had made fast and taken in the rope, the lady had no difficulty in climbing up to me, simply dancing up the dry rock in her rubbers and moving with style and authority. I had conceded, by the time she joined me, that she was obviously a very experienced climber, but as we were switching belays I felt a hand on my bottom, squeezing, stroking and then firmly laid on my thigh whilst I tied her into the belay. "Bloody hell!" I was scared stiff and shot off up the crack of the next pitch as if it were moderate in standard, not stopping to rest or to place my feet properly, simply cranking up on the large hand-holds. I reached a ledge beneath a thin crack and then obtained a good anchor up to which I brought once more my would-be seducer.

This time, when she reached my perch, I had almost to fight her off while changing stances. She pinned me against the rock and was kissing me, and then her hand was down between my legs and into my trousers. "Please, no, not here!" I was gasping and managed to break free. And then, not caring if she was holding my rope or not, I bolted off up the thin crack above, taking no time to look for a spike on which I might have placed a runner, and grabbing wildly at a huge exit jug, by which means I pulled over, and almost bounded up the easy finishing ridge of the pitch to stop on a sloping belay ledge above. I had climbed 50 feet of some of the hardest climbing I had led, and had hardly even noticed it!. I was shaking with fear as I took in the rope to bring the lady up. This time she did experience some difficulty in following, I was relieved to observe, and found it difficult to reach the finishing hold at the top of the crack. "Good," I thought, "that might take her mind off sex!" But no, as soon as she reached the ledge her hands were on me again, and this time she was undoing my pants and trying to pull them down, whilst I was trying to set off rightward along the ledge to gain the final crack and the easy finishing groove of the climb. "Please, no!" I insisted and, looking down, noticed that some walkers were watching us with obvious interest from the pub yard. "God knows what they will think is happening up

John Ramsden belayed, Dennis Gray climbing on *Laugh Not*, White Ghyll, Langdale, 1956.   Photo: J Brown

here?" I thought, as I at last broke free; but no, my pants were nearly down. I got angry. "Stop it, leave me alone! Please!" I was almost in tears as I pulled up my trousers and finally started out, so emotionally distraught by then that I nearly fell off whilst swinging left out of the crack to reach the final, easy groove. This led me to the top of the climb at a large terrace and, as soon as the lady had followed me up and safely arrived, I hurriedly untied my belay, not allowing her the chance to grab hold of me again. As it was her rope, I left her to coil it in solitude, on the big boulevard at the top of the cliff known as the *Oak Tree Ledge*. "Goodbye!" I had the decency to gasp out and she, in true ladylike fashion, waved me off with a free hand as I literally scampered off along the terrace. From there I scrambled down into Raven Crag gully and raced back down its screes to the Old Dungeon Ghyll Hotel, picked up my rucksack and legged it up to the Wall End Barn – my one aim to avoid being seen with her and identified as the two who had been locked in such passionate embraces on the ledges of the *Bilberry Buttress.*

I never mentioned the incident to anyone, but later that night, reunited with The Bradford Lads who had been away climbing on Pavey Ark, I ventured down into the Old Dungeon Ghyll bar, and there in a corner sat the lady artist. Completely unabashed she came over, embraced me and said, in a very meaningful way, to my friends, "Young Dennis led me up *Bilberry Buttress* today. He was wonderful!" At this remark many knowing looks passed between my older companions and, though they never mentioned it, I guessed that one or two of them had an inkling as to what had really happened – they may even have set me up, for I learnt later that, though the lady was a successful artist, she was also well-known for her fondness for young, male climbers. I was eventually to find out by experience that, as with many other things in life, sex is simply a fact of our existence, but there is a time and place for everything – and a Very Severe rock-climb in front of an audience is not exactly a good one.

When I started climbing, there were few guide-books to the popular climbing areas of Britain in print. In our home district of West Yorkshire, despite the fact that outcrops like Almscliff had been climbed upon longer than nearly any others, such detailed information had never been prepared. You therefore learned where the existing routes were by word of mouth and, as can be imagined, the history and details of first ascents and pioneering efforts were often sketchy. Many of the first ascents we made on our local outcrops in this period were later claimed by climbers preparing subsequent guide-books. In many cases our own ascents were not the first; it was obvious that they had already been ascended. I know of climbs which were

Bradford Lads with the Rock and Ice, Langdale, 1956. L to R: Doug Hayes, John Ramsden, Joe Smith, Eric 'Matey' Metcalfe, Marie Ball, Ray Greenall, Jim Lyons, Mike & Peggy Dawson.   Photo: Ramsden coll.

nail-scratched when I started to climb, and which appear as first ascents by later climbers who never wore nail boots in their lives! In such a situation rumour and myth can thrive, and we heard about many such climbing developments on the mountain limestone of the Pennines in the early 1950s.

A feature of those days, however, was that, despite not being in clubs ourselves, we were in touch with the other main activists of the day – The Creag Dhu from Glasgow, The Wallasey from Liverpool, The Sandstone from London and, of course, The Rock and Ice from Manchester. We met each other in the barns and dosses in the climbing areas, and thus from Ronnie Moseley, one of the Manchester-based group, I learnt about their pioneering climbs in Dovedale and Stoney Middleton in Derbyshire and their attempts on Kilnsey Crag in Yorkshire. Independently, Harold Drasdo and Keith King of our own West Yorkshire-based team tried to climb the latter in 1952 and enjoyed a minor epic best written about by one of those present; but I, along with an older climber, John (The Ram) Ramsden, decided to investigate the Rock and Ice routes, and to explore the possibilities for further new climbs. Ronnie had sent written descriptions of the routes they had made to me, and it was not true that these were all artificial, as some seemed to believe. It must be remembered that the only way then to protect many of these climbs was by using pegs, but the rock was

John Ramsden traversing the bridge in Glen   John Ramsden in 1956.   Photo: Gray coll.
Nevis, 1956.   Photo D Gray

mainly climbed free, a typical example being *Frisco Bay* at Stoney Middleton, which Don Whillans had pioneered and which we climbed during our visit, banging in pitons for protection with a Charlet hammer and using home-made pins borrowed from Arthur Dolphin, which were rather like a larger version of the modern RURP.

Stoney Middleton at this date was relatively unexplored, and we were very impressed by its steep, white limestone walls, pinnacles and cracks. Despite its situation looking out across a road to a working quarry, it was then a superb place to climb, for neither was it a litter dump, nor were the climbs polished horrors, as they are today. We looked around for pioneering possibilities, realising that this immense escarpment held the promise of many further climbs. For some reason, after walking all around the base of the crags, we seized upon the line of what is now *The Little Capucin* at the very far left-hand of the cliff.

The Ram was a good-natured giant who then worked in a foundry in Leeds and with whom I always felt safe, both climbing and travelling. He was a brilliant exponent of Chinese wrestling and I never saw him beaten in this minor martial art. Well over six feet in height, he towered over me and I often wondered what it would be like, trying to hold his weight if ever he parted company with the rock-face. At Stoney Middleton I was to find out for, having climbed up to a tree (long since disappeared) which grew out of the rock at half height and below the overhang of *The Little Capucin*, I belayed and brought him up. Handing over the piton hammer and the home-made pitons, we exchanged positions and he set out. After a mighty struggle he managed to get a piton in over the roof and, pulling on this, he cleared this obstacle. However, the top wall turned out to be loose and, cleaning as he climbed, he needed to put in a second piton. He was just about to clip his rope into this second peg when his left hand-hold broke – "Crack," off it shot, and "Shite!" he was off. Fortunately, the piton at the roof held; otherwise he might have decked out, for I had just given him some slack with which to clip his rope into the piton. We were climbing on a single, full-weight, nylon rope and when the jerk came on my waist, it pulled me hard against the tree. Grimly I held on with the rope tight in my bare hands. I had stopped him at some point beneath the roof but still above me, and lowering him back down to the belay was an agony as the rope ran through my flesh. The difference in our body weights was dozens of pounds and my ribs took a tremendous blow from the shock-loading of the rope around my lower back – they were sore for many days afterwards. "Up you go!" decided the Ram, pointing at me with a huge hand when I had lowered him safely down to my perch. I looked pleadingly at him for a moment but knew there was no arguing, for I had to at least give it a try!

In fact, apart from the loose rock I encountered at the top of the climb, it was a relatively simple matter of climbing up to, and then pulling up on, the two pitons that The Ram had hammered in. Typically for a man of such physical power, they were in to the hilt and needed much hammering from him to remove them. In the current list of first ascents (in the historical section on the crag) held on computer by the Peak District committee, it states that I was eleven years old at this date and had used ten pitons to climb the top pitch! I must write and put them right about that. However, amongst our friends in Yorkshire, The Ram and I did become known for a while as *Whack and Dangle*; for, after these first forays and with our newfound confidence engendered by our borrowed iron men and piton hammer, no unclimbed crack was safe from our attentions.

Our next undertaking was to visit Dovedale in Derbyshire. Just to get there from Leeds was an expedition via a train to Sheffield, a bus to Bakewell, then another to Ashbourne, followed by many miles of walking. When we arrived at our destination we were to be disappointed for, try as we might, we could not repeat Don Whillans' route – out over the roof of the cave of that marvellous pinnacle, Pickering Tor. This was no crack, but typical of The Villain, it was a bold piece of roof climbing for which I lacked the muscle and The Ram (he maintained) was too big. Our next experience of hammering in pitons was at Froggatt Edge, and it was to feel almost like taking candy from a child, inserting pegs into a straight crack line which already bore some marks of passage, but which we called *Piton Crack*. (It is now known as *Synopsis* and is, of course, a totally free climb.) We found out much later that it had been pegged already, a short while before our ascent, by Derek Carnell, Ray Wandley and Nat Allen, who were all to become my close climbing friends. Further emboldened, we then had a great scare pioneering a climb up the middle of the limestone slabs at Hawbank near Skipton.

Hawbank was then one of the finest pieces of rock of its type that I knew. It subsequently became very popular with local climbers in the late 1950s. Unfortunately, with the activities of the 'Quarry Lobby' growing ever larger, it has since been blown up, presumably to help make toothpaste for starving Africans and myself. It was about 140 feet high at its apex, and The Ram and I picked a line bang up the steepest, most intimidating part of the face. We felt very confident, for we reasoned that if the going got tough, all we had to do was bang in a piton!

This was all very well until The Ram, having ascended thirty feet from the ground, found in extremis that, although there were many crack lines, they were all blind, and he had no choice but to keep climbing up, hoping to find a placement to protect himself. Watching from the ground it all looked deceptively easy, for the slab was of a reasonable angle and seemed full of good holds. Eventually, at about 70 feet, The Ram reached a sink hole in the face of the slab, hammered in a piton and decided to belay. On following him I was to find that every hold sloped, that there were no incuts for the hands, and that within 30 feet my toes, inside black gym pumps, were aching from standing up on the rounded dimples in the rock, with hands being used only for balance. By the time I reached The Ram I was totally gripped, but was relieved to find he had a well-placed piton in for a belay. Above my head seemed a good crack and, taking over the lead, the piton hammer and the four pitons, I set out, heading for the fissure. On reaching it after 20 feet climbed by very trying moves, I was to find out that, like all other cracks in the slab, this too was blind and would not take our pitons. Only my faith in The Ram's immense strength kept me going, believing that, if I fell, he would hold me without any problem; I had not realised that, however strong he was, if his belay failed we would both be pulled off the slab. Once a leader falls, it requires good anchors to stop him, not just the strength of a single

Dennis Gray on the limestone slabs at Haw Bank.   Photo: Gray coll.

person's arms!

With this misplaced confidence, I somehow reached easy ground after about 40 feet of hard climbing, and scrambled to the top of the cliff via an easy rake. We were subsequently so full of hubris from our success that we decided the time had come to go for the big one – Kilnsey Crag – still unclimbed at that date. But even we were not so naive as to believe we could storm this great bastion with only five small hand-made pitons, and so The Ram decided that he would make a mould and cast as many pegs as we required during his lunch breaks at the foundry. Old bike frames, bits of scrap metal, steel wheels were all melted down, and the molten liquid poured into a mould. The resulting shiny pitons were the envy of our friends when we assembled them for our attempt.

Kilnsey Crag, set in Wharfedale, is a most impressive place. At its southern end it has a huge roof set high above the ground at about two-thirds of its 200 feet of cliff face. This huge overhang is the centrepiece of its challenge and is now climbed free (with in situ protection). But its buttresses lying to the west of this are, on close study, and despite the absence of any further large ceilings, almost equally impressive. We decided to tackle what seemed to us the best of these, The Central Wall, not believing the main roof to be climbable with the equipment we possessed. Our gear was just pitons, a single, full-weight nylon rope, steel karabiners and some slings.

If you could not free-climb a rock-face in that era, and had decided to resort to artificial means, you hammered in a piton, put a karabiner in its eye, clipped in and either got a sling into this and stood in it or, more usually, your partner held your weight whilst, half-suffocated by hanging on the rope, you tried to bang in another piton as high as you could reach above you. Our attempt took place in 1953, and by that date I had grown and was jockeying for position with my older companions. No longer the compliant, small boy, I wanted to share in the decision making, and so The Ram and I agreed that I would make the first attempt in the lead. Imagine a dated figure, seventeen years old, wearing a torn sweater, jeans and vibram-soled boots (more comfortable for standing in slings than gym pumps). And so, with The Ram still towering over me despite my growth, firmly holding the rope which was tied around his middle, I set forth up a crack-line in the Central Wall, banging in pitons as I climbed, hanging on the ropes, standing in slings, bedecked from my waist with an assortment of karabiners and the shiny, new pitons but also, fortunately, with Arthur Dolphin's old, mild steel pegs.

I made quick progress, for the crack was good and The Ram's pitons were a dream – you simply pounded them home and they seemed to slot into

First ascent Kilnsey Main Overhang, 1957. Ron Moseley climbing.   Photo: J Sumner

cracks as if they were made of blu-tack. At about 40 feet the crack closed for a section and I could not get any of the shiny cast pins into the small fissures that appeared there. Instead I placed one of Dolphin's pegs to the hilt and, confident in this, moved up, standing in a sling. The crack widened again and I continued to make steady progress, with a line of the cast pitons below me. At about 70 feet I tried to free-climb a section but found I could not solve the problem with which I was confronted, so I decided to drop back onto my top anchor, with only about a foot or so to lower. "Have you got me? I'm descending onto the piton." "OK!" I heard The Ram's assurance from the ground. I let go, expecting to drop only a few inches, but as soon as my weight came onto the cast piton, it simply snapped. "Jesus!" I was falling, and the next piton did the same, for, as soon as it was loaded, it just broke as if made of putty. I kept on falling and the pegs kept on breaking, one after the other. It was all happening very fast; my whole life did not unfold before me; but I was conscious of the ground coming up to meet me. I screamed, closing my eyes, expecting to feel pain any moment, but suddenly I came to a stop: the rope had me held a few feet above the deck, swinging in space, with badly bruised ribs, and almost strangling me in its embrace around my chest. Dolphin's piton had held me – the one I had placed at 40 feet – but I had fallen over 60 feet. How I blessed him, my father-figure; but how I uncharitably cursed The Ram as he lowered me the few feet to the ground. "You pillock, you nearly killed me!" For once my older, bigger partner let down his defences and said simply, "Sorry ... I hadn't known that cast pitons would not be safe!" I looked at him in disbelief, but then realised that I, too, knew absolutely nothing about such matters, and that The Ram's role in the foundry had not given him the understanding of how dangerous these pitons would be. A few minutes later we were falling around laughing at each other – I, safely back on the ground, chortling at my good fortune at still being alive, and The Ram at his stupidity. But it had really frightened me, and we decided to abandon our attempts to become famous by being the first to scale Kilnsey Crag.

It was to be five years before I returned for a successful climb of the Kilnsey Roof, along with Joe Brown and Harry Smith. This was only the third ascent, the honour of first having been earned by Ronnie Moseley in 1957, after a long siege. By that later date I had experienced many further epics and listened to a thousand and one stories whilst searching for wisdom in the steps of the fisherman – The Baron Brown!

Chapter Three

In the Steps of the Fisherman

The urban areas of northern England are, on first acquaintance, much alike – houses of red brick or stone, with their surfaces blackened by pollution from the factories in which most of their denizens once worked. But probe beneath the surface, and there is a great character difference between citizens of, say, Leeds, Newcastle or Liverpool that cannot be appreciated until direct experience changes one's perceptions. When I arrived in Manchester in February 1954, I had no previous experience of that city, but nevertheless knew and felt the pre-eminence its climbers then held in our appreciation of the sport's recent history. It is hard, now, for those not active at the time, to understand the impact that The Rock and Ice Club was then making, and what a legend Joe Brown had become since his modest beginnings, scrambling on Kinder Downfall only seven years before. Like the Arthur Dolphin story, the Brown tale is well documented, but even more so a veritable rags-to-riches, 'now't but pluck, a load of luck and his mother's washing line' rise to fame. This is, of course, a caricature, the real story being far more complex, its origins deeply rooted in the rigid class structures of the early 50s and the rapid change these underwent over the next decade.

At the age of 18 I was sent to Manchester by the Army to my posting, as a non-combatant, at the Pay Office in Stockport Road, Longsight, literally five minutes' walk from where Joe then lived with his mother in Dickenson Road. Gradually, at weekends during my national service, I began to go climbing with The Rock and Ice Club – a known fact amongst my friends at the Pay Office, and a connection which sometimes led me into difficulties. I was often pushed forward when someone was needed to scale heights to change a light bulb, or go up onto the roof to check for bombs or rescue stray cats. One morning 'C' company was lined up in the basement of the Army Pay Office and addressed by Lieutenant P. D. May, a wonderful Hooray Henry of an officer.

"Men, we have been picked for a special, top-secret assignment. The War Office has decided to test the security of RAF bases and we are to attack RAF Handforth tomorrow morning at 5am. We will go in disguise – blacken our faces with boot polish and cause as much disruption as we can. Everything is game, and I will issue you with thunder flashes and bangers, but, whatever you do, try not to get caught. The base is guarded by the RAF regiment with dogs. If they do catch you, mum's the word as to who sent you and which unit you're from! By the way, has anyone any idea how we might get over the wire into RAF Handforth?"

I stood there, determined to have no part in this madness, imagining what would happen if the RAF regiment caught me on an atom bomber base – they would probably shoot first and ask questions later. "Gray's our climber, Sir," blurted out Crilly, a scouse friend of mine, but not any longer.

"Are you, Gray? Good show! How do we get over the wire?"

"How high is it, sir?"

"I don't know – ten feet I would guess, and electrified!" postulated P. D.

"We could use one of those really high step-ladders, you know, the ones they use in warehouses. I have seen them fifteen feet high," I foolishly suggested.

Very early next morning we were picked up in an unmarked truck with a surprisingly large step-ladder strapped on its roof. To say that we looked like a team of commandos off on a desperate mission would have been an exaggeration – we were more like a troop of black-and-white minstrels on our way to a glee club with our blackened faces and assortment of old clothes. (P.D. May, I seem to remember, was in a cricket blazer, white flannels and, for some reason, a tin hat.)

It was a relatively simple matter to place the step-ladder over the perimeter fence and carefully climb over it. Once inside, and our step-ladder withdrawn, the action was classic. The RAF boys got the surprise of their lives as two thunder flashes erupted in their hut. Men came running through the doors or dived out through windows, half-dressed, naked, pyjama'd, screaming and swearing. Crilly, McCready and I made a runner for it across the tarmac to the RAF Handforth fire tender. With my friends' experience in hot-wiring we had it going in minutes, and then started the craziest drive of my life, up and down the runway, in and out of huts and offices, horn blaring, shouting abuse at the tops of our voices. "Bloody hell, this is as good as The Brass Bound Buggery Box," I was just deciding, when a bullet whistled over our heads. "Christ, they're firing at us!" Through the bottom of the vehicle's windscreen I could see some men of the RAF regiment, rifles at the ready, pulling triggers. "Let's get out of here!" I pleaded, but our escape route lay behind them. The regiment were brave lads and stood their ground, pumping shots over our heads until the very last moment, when they scattered as the fire tender bore down upon them. Once back up and over the ladder, however, we noticed that a man was missing in action – our leader, Lieutenant P. D. May, who was captured by the RAF regiment and interrogated for hours. We returned in our unmarked lorry without him and it took many phone calls from the War Office in London to get him released, for the RAF honestly believed we were a terrorist group, as P. D. bravely refused to talk, despite their threats and violence.

My climbing weekends with The Rock and Ice became more frequent and, from my first trips with them, I realised that their sense of humour and climbing standards were different from those of my companions back home in Yorkshire; as were their accents, which were rooted in Ardwick, Longsight and Levenshulme, three districts which made up an interlinked, run-down inner city area, which was then a forest of smoke-blackened brick houses. These Mancunians were more traditionally working class in their values and did not spend their mid-week evenings in arty-crafty activities, as some of my Bradford companions might do: Alfie Beanland, an artist – who was later to perish so tragically whilst attempting the second winter ascent of Zero Gully in 1958 – would occasionally, cash permitting, visit the ballet; Jim Lyons would read Plato; Harold Drasdo studied literature. They were also working class but, in 1954, there was a difference in cultural interests between the Grammar School educated kids, of whom I was one, and those who had been left behind by the eleven plus selection – the fate of most of The Rock and Ice members.

There is a well-known book about famous Mancunians and it has always been a mystery to me why it does not include The Rock and Ice members. In their own field they were as famous as, say, Christie, Renold or Dalton, and even The Happy Mondays, come to think of it. Certainly, they must have been as rich in character, diversity and achievement as most. However, this latter quality was not their goal when they first came together in 1951. As someone who knew them from the club's inception, I would give their raison d'être as more to do with seeking adventure, escaping from the smog and grime of their inner city environment and just having fun. Before I arrived in the Cotton Town in February 1954, I knew several of them well from meetings at outcrops, crags in Wales and the Lakes and in dosses such as Wall End Barn. They were the focus of many myths, most of which concerned the wonderman, Joe Brown. Usually, such stories do not maintain their aura of mystery once the person being lionised is exposed to public scrutiny. Then they are found to be not much better or not much worse than the rest of us, and the legend-making process moves on to the next victim. However, in Brown's case and also with The Rock and Ice this was not to be, for despite poor communications in the climbing world in 1951, and the time it took for the truth to become established, the Manchester group nevertheless emerged by common consent as a rare phenomenon. The only comparison I can really make is with events of a decade later in the pop-music industry with the appearance of the Beatles. They stood the whole of the sport on its head and somehow you knew that they were something special ...... although they themselves were unaware of this at the time!.

My earliest memory of one of these factual myths in the making was the time Arthur Dolphin and I visited Raven Crag, Thirlmere. It was raining hard, as it had been doing for days, and we were there only to look at the cliff's potential for it had only just been discovered by Alfie Beanland and Mike Dawson. Arthur intended returning as soon as possible to attempt some new climbs and, as we were walking along the road towards the base of the hillside below Raven Crag, we came upon a boulder which had recently been nail scratched – so recently that it could only have been climbed the day before. An impressive piece of work we decided, and subsequently tried to get up it. Arthur, who was climbing in tricouni-nailed boots, had to push himself to his limit. It was too hard for me and, though I tried my hardest, I could not climb it in my clinker nails. "Who do you think it was who has been up here in this weather?" I demanded in exasperation as I fell from the greasy rock-holds yet again. Arthur reflected a moment and smiled, "It must be Joe Brown!" I took this to be a joke, but later realised that he meant it. Sure enough, a little research revealed that he had been right. Arthur had met Joe, seen him climb, and immediately recognised that he was the outstanding climber of his era. It was typical of Dolphin that he would admit this, but many other people in the climbing world were initially not so magnanimous, especially those in the established clubs at that period. Slim Sorrell, Joe's constant companion in his early climbing years, was later to write: "They often appeared to resent our tattered and ill-equipped appearance at their local crags. That we invariably climbed at a higher standard only seemed to aggravate the position. Their pointless snobbish-ness was difficult to understand and we would avoid such groups whenever we could."

However, the Bradford Lads, myself included, were able to recognise that the emergence of The Rock and Ice group was something special, and that they were worthy of our respect. My first meeting with Joe Brown and Slim Sorrell at Wall End Barn did not disappoint my expectations as a fourteen-year-old, for they were not only impressive climbers but extremely good fun to be with, and long before I 'fetched up' in Manchester on national service I was to enjoy some adventures with them.

On one of our earliest trips down to Stanage Edge, The Ram and I dossed

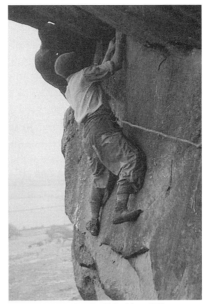

Slim Sorrell belayed, Don Chapman seated
and Val Brown climbing on *PMCI*, Curbar
Edge, in the early 50s.   Photo: J Brown

Joe Brown on *Finale Slab*, Almscliff.
Photo: D G Verity

with The Rock and Ice in a cave under a huge gritstone boulder in the
plantation. None of us had tents then and, in the absence of a barn, this nook
was our only shelter in the winter of 1953. Two of The Rock and Ice had
turned up one freezing winter's night to stay in this hovel, only to find
another climber wrapped up in his blankets and almost blocking the
entrance. For the next two days they climbed in and out of the cave over his
body, remarking each time that the guy was the soundest sleeper they had
ever come across. They actually nick-named him 'the dormouse'. On
Sunday night, packing to go home, they decided to rouse him and, in the
stygian gloom of the slit, shook him vigorously. It was only then that they
realised the poor bugger was a tramp who had frozen to death and been dead
for a few days.

On the Sunday morning of my visit with The Ram it was snowing hard
and not a good day for climbing so Joe Brown and Ron Moseley decided that
the time had come to investigate 'the pipes'. These turned out to be
concrete, about three feet in diameter and set into the ground nearby. "Let's
find out where they come out?" they decided. And so off we started, crawling
in unison along one of these shells – Joe, Ron, Ray Greenall and myself.

There was mud along the base of the pipes and a trickle of water coming slowly through. Within a few yards I was wet through and realised that there was no turning back, for it was easier to go forward than reverse, and it was impossible to turn round, so narrow was the pipes' diameter. After about a quarter of a mile I was beginning to panic, "Christ, they might go all the way to Sheffield or Manchester!" and then suddenly a thought hit me. What were these pipes supposed to carry? floodwater? It was snowing hard outside. "Get a move on!" It was Ron Moseley almost crawling over me, for we had no means of light. I scampered along as fast as I could and, being the smallest, I had more room for manoeuvre than the others. Faster and faster we crawled along, for I guessed that the others were also beginning to have their doubts about the wisdom of our exercise. Farther and farther we went into the darkness, bolstering each other with shouts of, "Yer big ninnies". Then, suddenly, it began to get lighter and it was no longer necessary to slide along by touch. Finally, we crawled out onto a hillside near Bamford, safely delivered, although wet through and covered in mud. In retrospect it was a bit of a crazy thing to do, but it was typical of the Manchester club: if the weather was not fit for climbing – and it had to be pretty dire – then they would usually find some other interesting and challenging diversion to appease their hunger for action. Many of these escapades became well documented over the next few years, such as riding down the Snowdon railway line sitting on a boulder; the speed that one could reach was impressive, depending on the state of the line – whether it was dry or wet, and how much oil was lying on its surface.

Many other challenges have still not appeared in print, one of these being an obsession with activities in and around fast-flowing rivers in winter. Castle Rock in the Lake District, once it had achieved popularity with The Rock and Ice for climbing meets and social events, was the scene of some of their more exciting activities. It was one of the group's favourite haunts from their earliest days, when they would bivouac at its foot amongst the boulders. Sleeping rough in the boulders at Castle Rock was an excruciating experience, for it was difficult to find any flat ground on which to lie, and there was one occasion when Joe camped on its summit with his harem – a club joke about the short period when he was still single but becoming famous, and had in tow not one but several young ladies. The Rock and Ice was then an all-male club, but they were never against encouraging women to join in their activities. In order to house them a large tent was borrowed, and the only place this could be pitched was on the summit of the crag, with the rest of the crew down below lying in their stone hovels. This really did fit in with the Brown myth which had him as an Oriental type, not from the cut of his clothes but more, his demeanour, temperament and physique. He was not, however, greedy about his good luck in enjoying such a surfeit of female company, and he did offer, on one occasion, to swap one of his brood for a duvet jacket!

It was on later trips to Castle Rock, when I was with the Army Pay Office in Manchester and in the ranks of The Rock and Ice (most of whom had by then purchased tents), that we turned to the river for adventure. Ropes would be slung above its deepest pools and foaming rapids, and you had to get across from one bank to the other, whilst the rest of the group bounced on the rope trying to flick you off into the icy cold waters. We did fall in on occasion, and then it was often a question of running the banks, trawling the flood with ropes or even diving in to rescue the drowning member. Joe used to hate getting wet and would adopt many dodges to avoid being ducked. He was as agile as a monkey on the ropes and somehow, at the last minute, as he was about to go under, would move at breathtaking speed back up the lines and out of danger. On one occasion he was still dry when all the rest of us were wet through and almost hypothermic. He had outmanoeuvred the would-be wetting team, but then Morty Smith and I dropped him into the middle of the river by the simple expedient of untying the ropes from the tree on the opposite bank. Morty and I were then the apprentices and our blind faith in Joe's abilities were such that we made no attempt to rescue him for, as Morty observed with the wisdom of his sixteen years, "He'll get himself out. Joe can swim like a fish!" He was, luckily, a very strong swimmer; but even he could not retrieve my van key a couple of years later when we were repeating this exercise. This was in 1957 when, as I was monkeying along the ropes, I dropped my ignition keys from my jeans pocket into a pool of fast-flowing water about ten feet deep. Every member of the club had a go at diving for them. Vin Betts, our limbo dancing champion (he once managed to get under a rope held only eighteen inches above the ground) nearly drowned in a determined attempt to retrieve them. He had dived in, got hold of the keys but, with cold fingers, had dropped them again into a fast-flowing rapid which swept him a hundred yards downstream.

And so, in the end, our hopes were pinned on the Baron Brown, our best swimmer, who had elected to try last. His mind would often produce an unusual solution to a problem, whilst climbing or in other situations. He decided on this occasion that I should hang upside down from the rope (which we had repositioned over the rapids where the key was now lying), held in place with slings and karabiners. Then I would hold Joe by his legs,

Joe Brown leading the first ascent of *A35*, Bamford Edge, 1958. 'Morty' Smith belaying. The route was named after Joe's vehicle, an Austin A35 van.   Photo: Don Whillans

'Morty' Smith leading *Elder Crack*, Curbar Edge, 1957.   Photo: W White

while we were slowly lowered by the others until he could reach the keys. This was working like a charm until I, too, went under, for the combined weight of the boys was insufficient to control that of Joe, me and the force of the rushing waters against his body. The effect of hitting the water made me let go and, once again, another Rock and Ice member shot down the river like a barrel going over Niagara. Fortunately, at this juncture, Valerie, Joe's wife, from a shopping trip in Keswick, otherwise one or more of us might have drowned, as attempts to retrieve the key were becoming ever more dangerous.

"Why don't you phone the RAC and ask them to get you a new key?" she demanded.

"I don't know the number and the van's locked," I responded, wet through and shivering with cold.

"It's stamped on the ignition lock," advised Pete Greenall, an engineer and always a bastion of common sense when all around him were not thinking clearly.

"I don't know how we'll get into my van," I wavered.

"You have to be kidding!" beamed his brother, Ray Greenall, pointing to his fellow Rock and Ice members with some pride. "These guys could get you into the Bank of England." And so it proved to be. The van door was opened in a trice by one of the Rock and Ice petermen, for a deprived youth in Longsight has to have some compensations!

These hunts for challenge and adventure when the weather was bad led The Rock and Ice into many unusual diversions: brick fights in the Llanberis Pass; stew-eating contests; rough game sessions; but one of the most impressive inventions was to put a rope across Gordale Scar near Malham and then cross The Scar on the rope. This was so far across that it required three 150-foot ropes to bridge the gap. Swinging across, protected by a sling and karabiners attached to the rope from your waist, was fine until you hit the knots joining the ropes. Then you had to hang there and unclip each snaplink in sequence until you were past the obstruction. Going down the ropes, as you set off, was easy, but from the middle onwards it was incredibly strenuous as you pulled yourself back up towards the opposite side of The Scar.

Obviously such antics aroused keen curiosity among locals and tourists alike, and I remember a photograph taken by one of them from the ground with a telephoto lens. It showed the late Eric Beard, wearing a topee and blowing a bugle, dressed in an old overcoat against the cold, hanging in the middle of the cleft. This appeared in the *Yorkshire Evening Post* the Monday evening after his crossing and was captioned, 'A rock climber in action at Gordale Scar this weekend'. Even in those far-off days climbers did not usually wear topees and blow bugles as they went about their sport.

Joe Brown might have occupied a special position at that time because of his climbing prowess, but in games such as barn rugby, which was a great favourite at Christmastime whilst staying at a farm in Wasdale Head, he was as likely to be given a hard time as anyone; and they played the game very hard indeed. On one occasion Eric Price had his nose broken, another member his fingers fractured; whilst I received a cracked rib in a head-on tussle for the ball with Whillans. But Joe was no ball player and so, when we organised games of cricket on a summer's evening on the Grochan field in the Llanberis Pass, he would be relegated to the outfield for, as his wife often told him, "Joe Brown, you have butter fingers!" There was always a questioning and never a blind acceptance of any kind of permanent pecking order. Whilst I, as the youngest until Joe Mortimer Smith joined, might always defer to Joe or Don Whillans over climbing decisions, the group would not accept their word on other matters – for instance, Joe was thought

Tyrolean, Gordale Scar.

Photo: Don Whillans

to be hopeless at running, and I would use this as a counter-challenge after suffering humiliation by his ease of ascent up routes that I struggled over. On being challenged to a race back down from somewhere like Clogwyn du'r Arddu, he would insist on being given a start, which became longer and longer each time I put him to the test, but racing either up to or down from the cliffs, I could usually win. He and some of the other club members, not being athletes, really had no idea just what a gap there was in fitness levels between someone in training like Eric Beard (240 miles of running each week) and top climbers like Don Whillans and Joe. They were supremely fit for the climbing standards of their era, but this made not a fraction of the physical demands on them that, even thirty years ago, was made on an outstanding fell-runner like Beardie.

Thus, on several occasions, differences of opinion on these matters led to serious challenges being made and accepted in what would now be called fell-racing. One Saturday in the spring of 1957 after a good day's climbing on Clogwyn d'ur Arddu with Joe and Morty, they both accepted my challenge to race them back to Halfway House, the small tea house on the Snowdon Railway that was run by Mrs Williams and her family. They demanded that I give them five minutes' start, as I was still in training and occasionally running for the Leeds Athletic Club along with Eric Beard. After packing away the climbing gear into our rucksacks, I watched them run off down the slope to the Llyn d'ur Arddu and then into the boulderfield around its rim. By the time the five minutes had ticked away, they were climbing the hill above the lake and still going well. I realised that I would have to go flat out to catch them if I was to beat them to the café and win my prize of a free brew there.

I set off at racing speed and, by the time I reached the Llyn, I had lost sight of them altogether. After puffing up the hill above it and then racing over the Maen-D'ur Arddu (the grassy slopes beyond), strewn with boulders and etched with little cliffs, I had them in my sights. I was closing the gap between us with every stride and was confident of catching them. But, in the act of gauging the distance, and still running fast around and in amongst the jagged rocks, I came without warning upon the edge of a small cliff. I had not realised that there were craglets of any height on the hillside, and was to find this out with a rude shock. My speed was such that I could not stop, and I decided to leap over the cliff, hoping that I could land safely at its base, picking a landing spot as I jumped. In mid-air I realised with horror that the base of this obstruction was littered with jagged boulders. As I landed, I hit one of them with my full weight bearing down on my left ankle. There was

such a sickening jolt that I passed out for a second. When I came to I was
lying on my back with my leg crumpled underneath me. "Help!" I screamed,
sitting up, "Help!" but I could see the two Joes still jogging away down
towards Williams'.

Finally they heard my screams and stopped, but stood there, obviously
wondering if this was some ploy to hold them up. I continued to shout, and
they must have realised from the tone of my voice that this was no joke. After
what seemed ages they about-turned and walked suspiciously back to where
I was sitting. When they reached me and saw my predicament, Joe observed
with a chuckle, as he and Morty helped me up to start carrying me down,
"You cunning little bleeder, you knew you couldn't have beaten us, so you go
and knacker your ankle to avoid having to pay for two brews. You Yorkshire
lads will do anything to avoid putting yer hands in yer pockets!" Perhaps this
incident gave the Baron a false sense of his running abilities for, at another
Rock and Ice meet, after some dispute about his athletic prowess, he had the
temerity to challenge the greatest fell-runner of his generation, Eric Beard,
to a real race. Beardie already held a string of records, and was to go on to
break almost every worthwhile challenge in the country until his tragic death
in a car crash in 1969. This contest was to be from the shore of Derwent
Water to the summit of Cat Bells, almost 1500 feet higher. Eric was to start
at the water's edge and Joe was to be given 'half a fell' start, commencing
from the halfway stage.

The organisation of this event took up most of a wet Saturday, which Joe
spent fishing – even in those days he was keen on this contemplative sport.
By late afternoon all was ready, the course marshalled by fellow Rock and
Icers and the contestants lined up. The prize was to be £5 paid by the loser –
a fortune to us then. All the rest of the club were confident that, with such a
start, Joe must win, and were making side bets on him. These I was happy to
accept, and I gathered in a great number of pledges of free brews and
cheese-and-tomato butties (a club delicacy) for I knew that, against Beardie,
Joe had not a cat in hell's chance.

"Go!" shouted the starter, Les Wright. "Go!" I repeated halfway up the
fell, catching the rest of the crew's signal. Joe had elected to run in his boots,
despite advice to the contrary from Beardie and myself and, as he puffed off
up the hill, his ever-present flat cap on his head, he looked like a contestant
in a fishing match who had mysteriously appeared at the wrong moment via a
time machine. Beardie, on the other hand, in his running vest and shorts,
wearing his Dunlop Green Flash running shoes, with his long arms, equally
long legs, barrel chest and immensely confident stride, looked like the tough

Eric Beard and Dave Gilmour during 'Beardie's' run from John o' Groats to Lands End.
Photo: D Gray

of the track. You could see the man was an athlete whilst Joe, struggling bandy-legged uphill, looked like he might do himself a mischief. Although I trained and raced with Beardie regularly at that period, he fooled even me. I had estimated that he would just pip Joe to the summit but, running with such speed up through the bracken-covered slopes, he passed Joe three-quarters of the way up. Once Beardie had run clear of him, Joe lost heart and simply stopped dead in his tracks, declaring, "I'm not the right physique for running, and in any case Beardie's a cheat because he has trained for the event and I haven't!" But he paid up later with a smile, for we were truly in awe after this exhibition of Eric's incredible uphill speed. I think this incident taught the Baron a lesson, for he never again took up a challenge which involved running.

On one of my earliest visits with the club to the river camp-site at Castle Rock, Don Roscoe arrived with an air rifle. He and Joe organised some target practice the next morning before we went climbing, and I was singularly unimpressed by the results for, although I was a non-combatant, I did secretly practise on the Army Pay Office rifle range. They were not good shots and the pellets went nowhere near the target, which was a can of beans set on a rock. "You're bloody hopeless," I informed them. Joe took this ribbing badly and said, "I bet I could hit you from a hundred yards!" I immediately took his bait. "I bet you bloody well couldn't hit a barn at twenty yards!" I confidently informed them, which annoyed Joe the more. "I'll show you! Here, put this rucksack over your head," he demanded, which, stupidly, I did, being confident that from a hundred yards he would not be able to hit me. The bag was put over my head; as far as I was concerned, only as a precaution against the off-chance of a fluke shot, and a pellet hitting my face, or particularly, one of my eyes. They led me across the field to my stance and then took up their positions at a point which was paced out 100 yards away. Unknown to me, they had stood me on the edge of a small jetty upstream from where we were camping, which was used by the local fishermen to launch their boats. "Ready?" enquired Joe, his voice sounding awfully faint from inside my bag. "Ready!" I assured him. "I'll aim at your legs, then, if I do hit you, it'll only hit your thigh!" "OK," I responded confidently. I heard the swish of the air rifle, and the next moment I felt a searing pain in my right thigh. Not only had the pellet hit me bang on target, but with a such a force that it went straight through my trousers and into my flesh. The pain was excruciating and I leapt up into the air with the shock of it, missed my footing and landed in the river, which caused me an even greater surprise. I quickly found out that trying to swim with my arms pinned into the rucksack over my head was impossible. I was going under and thought I was drowning when I felt two strong arms pull me out and then drag me up onto the banking. "You're a silly little bleeder!" Joe acknowledged as he pulled the rucksack off my head. "Now do you believe me? I told you that an air rifle could pierce human flesh." "Yes, you've made your point," I had to agree with some chagrin as I massaged my leg. "But why could you not hit the target before, when you were trying for that Heinz can from only 30 yards?" I demanded. "Because there is no bloody incentive in firing at a bean can," Joe laughed.

This may sound callous or cruel to the casual reader but, once a dare had been put down, you either accepted it or backed off. The Rock and Ice had this very challenging and competitive way of doing things, and I can remember once being at Froggatt Edge when they organised a 'follow-my-leader'. The leader, of course, was Joe, and wherever he went you had to follow: climbing solo up Sunset Slab, then down by Sunset Crack, hopping from boulder to boulder without touching the ground and then into Hawk's Nest Crack, up this and back down the adjacent Holly Tree Groove. No one forced you to follow and only your pride kept you going. The less able climbers like myself would back off as soon as we decided we were out of our depth, without any loss of face. It was a version of the children's game of Pirates, and it ended with us building a human pyramid up the then unclimbed Long John's Slab (later chipped into submission as was its more famous companion, Downhill Racer). The bottom tier of this edifice was made up of the big men of the club: Les Wright, Peter Greenall and Doug Verity; then, on their shoulders, the lighter weights, Ray Greenall and Eric Price; and on top of them the featherweights, Ronnie Moseley and I; and once into position, up over our bodies climbed Joe. I can recall being terrified as this swaying mass took the strain, and hearing everyone else laughing as if it was the safest construction in the world – such was the confidence that oozed from the group whatever mad scheme they took on. Joe had one of his feet on Ronnie's shoulders and another on mine. I felt as if I could not support him a second longer, when he decided to move up higher still onto our heads. Moseley took this without flinching, but I thought my head was telescoping into my body as he put his weight fully onto my pate. "Bloody hell, Joe, that hurts!" I complained, but the next moment it was all over and Joe had sprung off our heads for the top. Unfortunately, the hold he had reached was a loose flake which simply cracked under his weight, and the next moment he was coming back down like a cannon ball, landing first on Ronnie and me, and then the whole construction was down and falling. By a minor miracle Doug Verity, our gentle giant (a cricket professional in his other life), caught Joe and myself, one with each arm, stopping our fall and putting us gently to the ground at his side – this may sound a very tall story, but it did happen! Some of the rest of the lads were not so lucky, and they were strewn along the ground at the base of the slab, nursing various injuries. One of them, Peter Greenall, ended up in hospital with a fractured arm. Yet there was no moaning from the injured, for each of us knew that such activities were dangerous and that you could end up getting hurt.

Among the Rock and Ice, however, there was a certain compensation to be gained for injury in the shape of the Iron Cross. In keeping with the black humour of the club, you earned this by being the victim of a leader or solo fall. It was the real thing, a genuine ex-Wehrmacht job, and at the club's fortieth anniversary dinner the President of that year, Ray Greenall, was wearing it with great ceremony, for earlier in the season he had taken a tremendous tumble whilst climbing at Calpe in Spain. Whoever is holding it has to keep it until another member of the club has a fall, when it will mysteriously appear the following morning at that person's postal address – in an unmarked envelope with no message.

One of the most amazing escapes from injury by any of the Rock and Ice happened during a 'try driving whilst blindfold' challenge, taken up by Wilf

Ron Moseley leading the third ascent of *Cemetery Gates*, Dinas Cromlech, 1953.

Photo: Don Whillans

White. He was to drive blindfold down the Llanberis Pass in his ancient car – one of the kind that used to have a large front bumper and detached headlights – to which Mortimer, as the youngest and smallest member of the club, was tied with slings! Morty's task was to shout out the driving instructions: "Left hand down, right hand down, straight on," as the road unfolded. Wilf's blindfold was so well arranged by his challengers that he could not see a thing but Morty, tied on the front of the chariot, did not appreciate this. He did, however, have every incentive to make sure Wilf had a full and accurate flow of information. Morty, telling the story afterwards, recalled that, as they started down the hill the driving had been uncanny. They had bowled so quickly down over the Cromlech Bridge and through the bends of Ynys Ettws that he came to the conclusion, mistakenly as it turned out, that no one could drive like that when blind. And so, as they rolled into the next bend, he decided to test his theory and stopped shouting out 'left hand down, right hand down'. "I was convinced the bugger could see and that the blindfold had a slit in it." A moment later they went through the wall at the side of the road, with Morty hanging in the danger position, shouting his head off – but too late to correct their trajectory. Wilf had not been able to see a thing and really had been relying on his charioteer's instructions. By the greatest of good fortune Morty was unhurt, though slightly concussed when the rest of the Rock and Ice untied him. Unfortunately, the same could not be said for the car.

During the quickly changing social conditions that prevailed during the 1950s, climbing groups like The Bradford Lads, The Rock and Ice and the Creag Dhu, although still poor materially, were finally able to afford their own transportation. Initially, this was in the form of motor-bikes and, later in the decade, it was to be vans. These latter were almost universal by the end of the period, but the motor-bike was by common consent the most exciting method of travelling to and from the climbing areas. My original climbing friends, The Bradford Lads, had found this out the hard way, and the number of crashes and fractures they sustained over about a three-year period would almost have kept a private medical clinic in business. The Rock and Ice replicated this and had several impressive pile-ups, including one in the Idwal Valley when about half a dozen club members came off at the same bend. However, my own narrowest escape in the mid-fifties was whilst riding with my old climbing buddy, The Ram. It occurred shortly after I had returned to Yorkshire after completing my national service.'

We had been climbing one Wednesday evening at Ilkley, and afterwards had stopped off at the nearby Cow and Calf Hotel. In those days there was a

Charlie Vigano with his 1000 cc Vincent 'Black Shadow', Langdale in the mid-50s.
Photo: Vigano coll.

torch singer, a Madam Eli Reinhart who used to perform there in cabaret, and The Ram had gone all sentimental on this well-preserved piece of mutton, dressed up and passing off as lamb. We stayed on the evening in question until late into the night, my companion drooling over every wiggle of this lady's hips, whilst she shimmied and sang her way around a small stage. When the bar closed we set off on the Royal Enfield Bullet down a winding back road which would lead us down to Burley Woodhead, driving as if we were in the TT. We hit the Z bend just before Burley with The Ram singing his heart out, repeating Madam Eli's last number – 'Wanted someone to love me' I believe it was called. I realised with horror as he put the bike on its ear, leaning it into the bend, that there was oil on the road. I screamed "Watch out!" and then we were over. In retrospect I was lucky, for I did a double somersault right across the road and landed on the grass verge, winded but unhurt. The Ram was not so fortunate, for the bike took him with it, crashing and bouncing down the road, and, when it fetched up, we found that one of his legs was fractured. Thinking about this now, I must have been incredibly lucky in that motor-bike era, for that was the fifth such crash from which I escaped unhurt, whilst my companion ended up in

Neville Drasdo leading *Waleska*, Ilkley in the 50s.   Photo: W Todd

hospital.

Later we were to find that travelling by van could be equally dangerous. One Friday night, a short while after The Ram had recovered from his crash, we were on our way to North Wales on the repaired 'Bullet'. Just as we entered the notorious 'Betws Bends', a small vehicle overtook us as though we were standing still. The inevitable happened and the van, having just missed us, proceeded to cannon along, hitting walls, lurching from side to side, whilst its driver fought to regain control. We followed its progress with horror and fascination. When it finally came to rest it looked like a child's pram. We stopped to help, guessing that they must be climbers, and, as we ran up to the scene, the driver and his front passenger were just crawling unhurt out of the wreckage. But from the back of the van, trapped under a collapsed roof, we could hear a low moaning. "Good God!" I thought, "I know that voice." I had recognised it as belonging to Ray Greenall. "Ray, Ray, are you alright?" "Course I'm not, yer daft bugger! Get me out!" When we did it was obvious that his arm and collar bone were shattered. "What were you doing in that van?" I enquired as we were waiting for an ambulance, for it was obvious from their reactions that Ray hardly knew his driving companions. "Just cadging a bloody lift," he painfully informed me.

In those times of rapidly changing social conditions, our camping arrangements also became more comfortable, at least compared to what we had enjoyed when staying in barns and caves. We could now afford tents and decent down sleeping-bags; we had primus stoves and, despite being traditionally working class and used to having our mothers, sisters or other women-folk doing the cooking at home, at weekends we would set to and cook hot meals for ourselves, working in the confines of a small two or three-man tent. We did, however, have several explosions when primus stoves erupted due to being over-pressured or blocked; but luckily no-one was badly burnt on these occasions. I was camping one night below Cloggy when my tent companion knocked a candle over and set fire to the fabric above our heads. We just managed to scramble clear as a strong wind fanned the flames into an inferno within a matter of seconds. It is still a source of incredulity to me how quickly our tent burnt down. Fortunately, two others were camping there that night, and four of us were crammed into a small two-man tent to await the morning, when we could begin salvaging the charred remains of our equipment. By today's standards our tents were very badly designed. My tent, not having a sewn-in groundsheet, blew away from above our heads in a gale whilst we were camping in the Grochan field one Saturday night. Fortunately, a member of the Vagabond Club, Jimmy O'Neil, found it wrapped around a telegraph pole in Nant Beris, about a mile away, from where he had been setting out to go climbing. Having guessed that it belonged to someone camping at the Grochan, he came up to where we were lying out in the open, clutching our missing cover. A similar occurrence happened when I was camping with Joe and Morty in the same field in 1957. The Baron used to be very proud of his tent, a single pole job with a separate groundsheet, which looked a bit like a red Indian's tepee. It was a wet Sunday, an absolute hurricane of a wind was blowing, and everybody else had either had their tents blown over or had pulled them down, weighted them with boulders and cleared off to shelter elsewhere until the storm abated. Meanwhile, we continued to sit it out under the tepee. "Bloody soft ninnies!" The Baron commented on the frailties of our fellow campers from the depths of his sleeping-bag, whilst Morty pumped the stove and I clung onto the single pole, becoming increasingly worried that, at any moment, not only would the wigwam go from above our heads, but we would go with it and be carried away and smashed into the rocks on the edge of the camp-site. "Bloody hell, Joe, don't you think we should try to pack up?" I nervously enquired. "This tent will stand up to anything ," he was assuring us, just as an extra strong gust came, ripped under the sides of the tent, despite all the boulders we had piled onto its sides, and swept away the top cover. Like an unfolding umbrella it disappeared into the leaden skies, leaving us lying in the open on the groundsheet. I had just been reaching for a full bottle of milk to hand to Morty for our tea when the blow came. The blast was so incredibly strong that it tore the bottle from our hands, and we could only watch as the tent fabric shot into the skies in the direction of Llanberis. The next moments must have been like a pantomime as we rushed hither and thither trying to collect our possessions as they blew here, there and everywhere in the screeching wind.

They used to have a saying in The Rock and Ice: "If you have any weaknesses the boys will find them." Any foible, mannerism or affectation would be quickly scented and then ruthlessly parodied to the point where a burlesque developed before your eyes. Particularly adroit at this were Nat Allen, Ronnie Cummaford and, of course, Slim Sorrell, who had been Joe's earliest regular climbing companion. Slim loved wild activities such as organising brick fights, wrestling matches and eating competitions, and he was no respecter of reputations or bruised egos. A bear of a guy, his great love was Western movies and books. When I first moved to Manchester, he and his wife Dorothy were extremely kind to me. I used to go on mid-week evenings to their house for meals, and to enjoy the luxury of perusing Slim's extensive library of Western paperbacks. 'Sudden' was his big hero, and he used to relive the plots of these books at weekends, when he would give a demonstration of how the hero outdrew his foes. Slim, against all appearances, was actually a policeman, and because of this he specialised in unarmed combat. Once, when Joe and others from The Rock and Ice were with him at Dovestones Quarry, he offered to teach them how to do an 'Alf Bridge' break-fall from a ledge high above the ground, explaining that it was a useful technique for the group to know about if ever they parted company with the rock-face. "There's nothing to it. You dive off and as you hit the ground, you simply roll forward!" "Show us then!" demanded his unconvinced audience. "OK! OK!" Slim dived off and unfortunately miscued, landing awkwardly on one leg, which fractured.

Of the early Rock and Ice members who are now dead, Slim's demise was perhaps the saddest and certainly the most dramatic. It occurred in November 1975, when he had been called upon, because of his police experience in dealing with young offenders, to attend a course in child care at Cardiff City College. A man called Nesbitt, who was later found to be mentally unstable, entered the college carrying a sawn-off shut gun and was terrifying other students. Slim decided to humour him and agreed to go for a walk with him to discuss his grievances but, as they walked out of the building, Nesbitt shot him at point blank range, and Slim died a short while later from the wounds he had received. It was a terrible fate for someone we knew as a friend, and a lover of life to the end. Every time I eat a bowl of stew, pick up a stone or see a Western movie, I think of Merrick 'Slim' Sorrell. Unfortunately, his story did not end with the goodie and his lightning fast draw beating the odds that were stacked up against him.

Joe Brown's 'weakness' that was parodied by The Rock and Ice was the burden of fame that he had to carry. This provided a source of great amusement to the group, and thus a thorn in Joe's side: he had to bear a good deal of irreverent baiting. I recall waiting at Joe's house one winter's night with Eric Beard, while The Baron packed his gear before we set out for Ben Nevis. When the 'phone rang he shouted for us to answer and Beardie picked up the receiver. "Joe Brown's residence," he intoned, in his best butler voice. "Say, that's just great, man, this is the manager of Joe Brown the singer. We've been thinking what a great publicity stunt it would be to get together the three Joe Browns: Joe the climber, Joe the boxer and Joe the singer." (The boxer was then an American world light-heavyweight champion.) Beardie was gobsmacked by this information and said simply, "Hang on a minute," and then went to relay the news to an equally surprised Joe Brown the climber. "Tell him yes, but the meeting must be up on Ben Nevis where we will be climbing in the cold snow and ice for the next week," decided The Baron. Beardie picked up the receiver once more and reiterated Joe's decision to the singer's manager. Sitting in an armchair beside the phone I could anticipate the man's reaction and overheard his spluttering confusion. Beardie decided to try to be helpful. "Has Joe Brown the singer ever done any climbing?" he enquired. "No, but he's a good tennis player!" Eric passed on this piece of information to us and we immediately fell around Joe's living room in hysterics, chorusing at Joe, "Anyone for tennis!" Needless to say, Joe Brown's manager rang off in high dudgeon, and I do not think the Longsight idol heard any more from him.

We used to like retelling this story whenever Joe was around simply to redress the balance, for the media were creating a load that was hard for him to bear. Particularly difficult must have been 'The Human Fly' tag. One morning, around the time of his move to open his climbing shop in North Wales, I caught sight of an arresting headline in one of the more seedy tabloids: "The Human Fly moves to Llanberis!" I found a postcard with an appropriate picture on the front and sent it addressed simply 'To the Human Fly, Llanberis'. Amazingly, it reached Joe safely the next morning.

One hears much talk these days of the 'swinging sixties', for that was the decade of The Beatles, The Rolling Stones and The Who. It seems that no one ever tells their kids, "You should have been around in the fifties – that was where it was at!" But, in climbing terms, I cannot think of another decade in which so much was happening, with the Creag Dhu, The Bradford Lads, The Rock and Ice and similar groups breaking barriers in climbing standards. In Britain they were the history-makers, but further afield in the Himalaya there were the epoch-making first ascents of Annapurna, Everest, K2, Kanchenjunga and Nanga Parbat. In the United States there was the first climb of The Nose of El Capitan in Yosemite, and in the European Alps, outstanding super routes on the Drus, the North Face of the Droites, and the Eckpfeiler Buttress of Mont Blanc. The great foreign climbers of the period were Buhl and Bonatti, and what an impression they both made on the attitudes of young climbers everywhere, their ascents being almost quixotically pure. I could postulate that Hermann Buhl had a greater influence on British climbers than any other single person, except for Joe Brown. Joe was unique – the colossus of the 1950s for all those who knew him, climbed and socialised in his company. He was the greatest climber any of us had ever seen, but he was also a friend. Although he was no saint, he was by turns funny, witty, cunning, clever, competitive, obstinate and wise, but always truly humble. In The Rock and Ice it was known that whenever we tossed a coin with him – for deciding tasks like who had to make a brew, lead a pitch or carry a rucksack – he would always insist on

Joe Brown at Tremadoc.   Photo: D Gray

using his own penny, which we believed was double-headed. We knew it was not, but such was his luck, for he won on nearly every occasion, making you happily believe in yet another of the myths. He was rivalled in the 1950s only by his younger and more aggressive partner, Don Whillans, and together they formed the strongest partnership in the history of British climbing. Happily, The Baron is still active and, in his sixtieth year, was able to lead *Suicide Wall* at Cwm Idwal on a cold, windy day, and also to reach the summit of Cho Oyo, the eighth highest mountain in the world. Of such achievements are the legends made!

Chapter Four

Simply Whillanesque

Don Whillans, unlike most of the other Rock and Ice members, was not from Manchester but from Salford. The undiscerning might think of them as the same place, but not those with intimate knowledge of the area. Lower Broughton was the place where The Villain grew up during and after the last war, and it was at that time rougher even than Longsight or Levenshulme, matched only by Ardwick in dereliction, for it was also a jumble of grimy brick terraces. Being unusually small, Whillans learnt from an early age in that inner city environment to fight for his rights against bigger, but rarely stronger, kids. Unlike Brown, he was a games player and loved sport, particularly gymnastics. By the time he was eighteen he had the physique and temperament of a pocket-sized Hercules, which quickly won for him an unusual reputation for ferocious climbing and equally aggressive behaviour off the crags.

I first met him at Whitsuntide in 1951 when he was seventeen and I was two years younger. He was walking up to Cloggy on his own as I was walking down and, as he drew level, I got the impression of someone who chewed nails and spat rust. Fair-haired, sporting a small quiff over a boxer's face, he had a wedged-shaped body only as big as mine (then at 5'3") but obviously twice as powerful. He stopped in his tracks and stared hard at me for a moment, and with a withering look came out with an, "Ahh-doo!" as a greeting. I stood transfixed, unable to catch properly this utterance.

"Ahh-doo!" he slowly reiterated.

I could see by his demeanour that his temper was rising and stammered out an "Hullo," then turned and bolted down the Llanberis track.

"Bleeding stuck up!" I heard him spit out as I took flight. I was not allowed to forget this incident when next we met. This was the following Easter when I joined a Rock and Ice bus trip to Glencoe. He was my seat companion and I had to suffer the full brunt of his spikiness and caustic wit.

By the time I arrived in Manchester in February 1954, Whillans had become one of the most talked-about characters on the British climbing scene, and only Brown himself was more of a legend. Even this balance was to change and, from thereon until his death in July 1985, Don remained centre stage in that respect, for the stories of his adventures proliferated and became folklore to climbers in many parts of the world. Some were undoubtedly exaggerated, whilst others are known only to a few intimates or to those present at the time. I recount only those I know about either first-

Don Whillans relaxing at home in Crawshawbooth, 1963.
Photo: J Darby courtesy Mrs Audrey Whillans

hand or from Don's own side of the coin. Some are not to his credit, but of
all the Whillans traits perhaps the most significant was that he cared not a fig
about public opinion. If you were his friend, and I counted myself as being in
that category, you accepted him as he was, since he made no allowance for
your sensitivities either in his language or behaviour.

Shortly after I arrived in Manchester, one of the great Whillans
confrontations occurred. One Wednesday night, after we had been to the
Levenshulme Palais de Danse, he had the first of several run-ins with bus
conductors. Why Don and crew members of the Manchester Corporation
Transport were an explosive mix, I cannot now explain. However, on the
first such occasion, he was climbing the stairs to go onto the top flight of a 92
Corporation double-decker, when the conductor made some rude remark
about Whillans, because he had dived onto the vehicle before it had properly
stopped and set off up the stairs immediately, which meant that the
conductor had to follow The Villain upstairs to get his fare. On hearing this
oath, Don came back down and offered his money, but not without a
typically acerbic comment to the effect of, "That's what yer get paid for,
mate!" This was more than the conductor could take, for it later transpired

that he and his driver were well-known in their own circles as hard men. In fact, he was the infamous Bully McTeague!. This meant nothing to the young Whillans, who took great exception when the Bully, still swearing, suddenly made a grab at him, a manoeuvre which Don anticipated and, lashing out with a fist just as the 92 accelerated, got the added impetus of several tons of metal behind his blow. This had a dramatic effect, which even Don had not anticipated, for the conductor shot off the bus and landed on his bottom in the road. The bus driver had seen what was happening through his mirror and, slamming on the brakes, jumped down out of his cab, ran round and picked up his battered colleague, who amazingly was unhurt. Meanwhile, Don stood on the bus platform, awaiting their onslaught like Horatio. This not only came at him frontally but also from behind, for as he lashed out at the Bully and his mate, some of the passengers came down the stairs and decided to join in.

Thus the battle took form, and slowly Don was driven down the lower-deck aisle of the bus. During his retreat before heavy odds, the sneaky bus driver climbed in behind Whillans through the emergency door, set immediately in front of the driver's cab. The Villain was having a hard enough time already, for no sooner did he fend off one would-be attacker, than another one took his place. Driven slowly down the bus gangway by the sheer persistence of their attack, he was suddenly seized by the bus driver from behind and both his arms were pinned. "Crash, smash!" Bully McTeague laid into him and landed two crushing blows into his face.

When telling the story the next night in the Manchester YMCA, Don, who looked as if he had been run over by a tractor, declared that he thought he was about to take a real beating when he managed to get a hand free and, reaching down behind him, grabbed the bus driver's testicles. "Bully, he's got me balls!" he screamed, as Don wrenched with all his might and was let go, at which Don managed to fight back and knock McTeague down. But then, once again, he felt himself grabbed from behind with both arms pinned to his sides. He was just about to try to repeat his previous manoeuvre, when he heard the unmistakable words: "Hello, hello, what's going on in 'ere?" It could only be a British Bobby, and so it was: the strong arm of the law. "Now then, sonny, what's this all about?" demanded the policeman who, like the driver, had clambered in through the emergency door. Subsequently, despite the protestations of the crew and the passengers, he could not bring himself to believe that this one small youth could have caused so much havoc. And with an avuncular, "Now you run along, son, and keep out of trouble in future," he dismissed Don to walk the rest of the way home.

There was a sequel to this first bus punch-up for, a few days later, Don was at his parents' home in Lower Broughton when there was a knock on the door. In the house alone that night, Don answered the knock, and there before him stood one of the biggest men he had ever seen. "Is your father in sonny?" he demanded. "Err, no, he's out. What do you want him for?"

"I've come to fight him. He attacked me brother on a bus the other night, and he must be a real hard man, for nobody normally gets the better of us McTeagues!" Whillans stood there, incredulous for a moment, for his dad would not have hurt a fly, and then the truth dawned.

"It was not me Dad that was in the fight with yer brother, it was me! I'll fight you if yer like!" The guy on the doorstep gasped in utter disbelief, for Whillans only came up to his midriff.

"It was you! You! Bloody hell, our kid must be getting soft! If a little bugger like you beat him up, he deserved it!" And he wandered off, still shaking his head in disgust. This and several others such incidents were the beginnings of the Whillans hard man tag, and earned him his nickname, 'The Villain'.

At that time, Don was an apprentice plumber and had to work Saturday mornings, so that he tended to miss some of the Rock and Ice activities, but he owned a motor-bike and usually arrived at the weekend venue, Saturday afternoon or evening. Then he was a great enthusiast not only for climbing, but also for the inevitable games sessions. In those days he neither smoked nor drank, and it was only with great reluctance that he would attend the pub with the rest of the crew, preferring to stay either in the barn or in his tent. On a Sunday morning, incredible as it may seem now, he would often refuse to go climbing until he had listened to the omnibus edition of the Archers on a small radio he would bring out specially for this purpose. He listened avidly to this farming soap opera, and if he had missed an episode during the previous week, he would insist on waiting until he had heard this before setting off for the crags.

The Rock and Ice games were barn rugby, hanging one-fingered off a nail driven into a beam, press-ups, pull-ups, wall squatting, gymnastic feats – the same challenges that Dolphin and his generation had been so keen on. Whillans was not the strongest person in the club, for that was definitely Morty Smith who, along with Moseley and Whillans, earned for the group the title of 'The Little Men'. Morty could press up easily with me sitting on his back a dozen times and more, but Don was the most agile. He could jump and leap phenomenally, and I once saw him climb up *Short Slab* at Curbar Edge in his Alpine boots and then, instead of walking round, jump

Don Whillans on the Grade VI slab, East Face of the Grand Capucin, 1955.
Photo: Mrs Audrey Whillans

back down from the top. He used to like jumping off the Froggat Pinnacle onto the hillside behind, a feat which Morty tried to emulate; but he misjudged his landing and fell down the gully at the monolith's side to land, after bumping and falling over thirty feet, bruised but unhurt at its base.

Joe Brown and other club members enjoyed playing cards, and liar (poker) dice at weekends, but this was not for Don. He was into the physical challenge of climbing, and in the evenings when we could not climb he really entered into the spirit of the games sessions. Teams would be picked, and I used to be really worried if I was not on his side, for he played barn rugby as hard as anyone I have ever met. If you had the ball he went for you as if his life depended on it, but woe betide you if you were on his side and he thought you were not giving your best! It is intriguing now to gauge how strong some of The Rock and Ice were in that era by comparison with today's superfit rock athletes. Most of them worked in manual jobs, and therefore had no need to spend hours a day pumping iron to keep fit, for they carried heavy loads of building materials, lead, fireplaces and bricks all day long. Some of them could do one-arm pull-ups (in Morty's case with either hand), and many dozens of press-ups. I have never met any modern 'rock jock' who can do all the group's individual physical feats, from Joe Brown's bum skipping or Whillans' ability to jump his own height from a standing start, to Thos Waghorn's ability to put both legs behind his head (at once), as could Brown. The most impressive of all these challenges, however, was Morty's trick of standing up from face down flat on the ground, with a man sitting on his shoulders. He could do this every time, but in order to emulate this feat, I saw Don cut his head badly and emerge bleeding but triumphant, standing with his pay-load safe in the final piggyback position. He never managed it again in my presence, despite many other attempts.

In those early Rock and Ice years Whillans could be the most difficult of persons to deal with, and some of the other club members such as Ron Moseley and he were not always on the best of terms. The rivalry over the first ascent of *The White Slab* on Cloggy is well-documented elsewhere; of how Moseley snatched the climb the day before Don intended making his attempt, but, all in all, it is remarkable how forbearing most of the group were in not responding to either his sarcasm or temper. The bonds of friendship established in hard climbing situations were usually more telling than temporary disputes. However, I can remember being absolutely amazed on the very first occasion I witnessed Don lose his rag. This occurred on Dow Crag, above Coniston in the Lake District, when he was climbing with Morty and me, the apprentices.

Johnny Cunningham (left) and Don Whillans playing deck tennis on the boat from Liverpool to Bombay, 1957.   Photo: Mrs Audrey Whillans

He was leading up the second pitch of *Eliminate B*, and it was a fine winter's day, although a little chilly. In order to keep warm Morty, who was on the ledge alongside me as I was holding The Villain's rope, was bouncing away on his belay, jumping up and down and singing his heart out. "Oh, yes, I'm the Great Pretender!" he was chanting, when two climbers appeared on the scree at the base of the climb and shouted up to us, "I say, you up there!"

"Who, us?" I responded above Morty's singing. (He was actually quite good at it.)

"Yes you! Have you such inferiority complexes that you can only climb by making such a noise?" the tallest of the scree-bound figures declaimed up at us, in what is best described as Oxbridge dulcet tones.

"Err, no! Sorry. Morty, perhaps you'd better tone it down a bit?" I suggested to my younger partner.

"He'll do nothing of the bleeding sort. Morty, keep on singing!" came the command from our leader above, now bridged across a steep wall and angrily eyeing the figures on the scree below. Morty did as he was told, his voice rising in power and, once again, from down below came the response, "You lot up there! I say, did you not hear what we said? Have you such inferiority complexes?" He got no further, for a shadow from above me was climbing down with the speed of an athlete, and then going on below me so fast I could not keep pace in paying out the rope. It was Whillans who, as he climbed down, was shouting out a torrent of abuse.

"Stop where yer are. I'll bleeding show you who has an inferiority complex, yer stuck-up bleeders." I was flabbergasted. I had never seen anyone in such a temper in my life; the aggression was bursting out of him at every move, and within minutes he had climbed down a hundred feet, untied and was running across the scree towards the astonished climbers. They stood their ground until he was only a few feet away, but then they must have realised their imminent danger, for there could have been no reasoning with that flat-capped tornado, and they took flight.

He chased them across the scree, taking great swipes at their backsides with his boot-clad feet, just missing them on several occasions. The last we saw of them, they were disappearing down the track to Coniston, whilst Don, having seen them off territorially, about-turned and walked slowly back up to the foot of *Eliminate B*, re-tied on the rope and then climbed up to us in total silence, his anger completely abated. "Watch the rope," he grunted as he went past us, climbing easily and fluidly up the rock-face, whilst Morty continued to sing and I to stare at him in total, open-mouthed amazement.

Whillans was a great enthusiast for rock-climbing in Scotland, correctly identifying the fact that, in the 1950's, new route possibilities north of the border were boundless. Unfortunately, with limited holidays and the often prevailing bad weather, he was foiled in achieving the quantity of new routes that his talent deserved. However, some of his innovations, such as *Sassenach* and *Centurion* on Carn Dearg, are now classics.

We heard about the Etive Slabs on the South Face of Beinn Trilleachan; their first route was pioneered in 1954 by Eric Langmuir and they were described as oceans of unclimbed granite hundreds of feet high, the biggest sweep of slabs in Britain. And therefore, one Easter break, Don, Audrey, Ron Cummaford, Morty and I headed north to rendezvous in Glen Etive with Hamish MacInnes in order to explore them for ourselves. When we arrived the weather was atrocious, and it never stopped raining for the whole of our four-day holiday. Despite trudging, each day, up to the foot of the slabs from the bothy in which we were staying at the end of the Glen, we achieved little, having to retreat from each line we attempted. One such descent by Whillans was dramatic for, climbing in boots, he had managed to get about forty feet up what later became the first pitch of a route called *The Long Reach*. Water was streaming down the slab and it was raining hard. It soon became obvious to Morty and me, belaying him on the ground, that The Villain was not going to make it, for his feet were shooting off the

Chris Bonington and Don Whillans at Kleine Scheidigg, 1961.
Photo: courtesy Mrs Audrey Whillans

friction holds as if he were wearing roller skates. For some reason it took us a
while to realise that the Etive Slabs could only be climbed in reasonable
conditions, and that they demanded friction climbing on dry rock.

"Watch me, I'm going to jump off!"

"Is that wise Don?" I timidly observed.

"Wise? What do you bleeding suggest – wings?" he acidly observed from
above my head.

"Err – no!" and the next moment down he came; and somehow managed
to turn around and run down the slab, sliding, slipping, but upright. Morty
and I grabbed him as he landed, and the force of his descent knocked us
flying, leaving Don unhurt at the bottom of the rock-face, but Morty with a
bruised hip and me with a sprained wrist.

MacInnes did not accompany us on these fruitless trips up to the Slabs,
preferring to wander off exploring amongst the bens and glens surrounding
Loch Etive, then an unspoilt and relatively unfrequented region of the

Highlands. I can remember being very impressed by Hamish's ability at wood-cutting and fire-building, for each evening, despite the terrible weather, he would build a large fire on the loch's shore for us to sit around. He had a double-headed axe, which he had won in a logging competition in the antipodes, and he used to be able to cut through a tree trunk the circumference of my body in a single blow. Morty and I spent hours trying to emulate this feat without success and, despite Hamish patiently explaining that it had nothing to do with strength but was more a matter of technique, we went away from that Easter trip convinced that the man was inordinately strong.

Each day, as we walked up to the Slabs, we argued about whether the water in the loch was salt or freshwater, and Ron Cummaford – one of the wittiest, funniest guys on the climbing scene, who often got the better of Don in verbal exchanges – played this puzzle for all it was worth. On the final morning of our stay in Glen Etive it was still raining and so, as we set off on yet another journey to the base of the Slabs, Whillans decided he would solve the water question once and for all. As we walked past the shores of the loch with Ron in attendance, he climbed out onto the edge of the old pier. (In the 1950's David MacBrayne steamers occasionally called here with the odd cargo of tourists on their West Highland cruises from Glasgow). See Glen Etive and die! At least, that is what nearly happened to Don.

From a safe distance, Cummaford urged the Villain on.

"Look Don, there are some steps down from the pier to the water. If you climb down those you will be able to reach down and taste it!" It mattered not that a gale was howling down the loch and the pier was being washed by giant waves (which reminded me of the Blackpool of my boyhood when my Dad was there playing the theatres and clubs). And so Whillans climbed down the steps, watched by Morty, Audrey and me from the hillside above the loch. 'Crash!'... The wood must have been rotten to its core, and the whole lot collapsed. The steps simply disintegrated as Don descended and, "Bloody hell!" he was down into ten feet of icy cold water. We ran over to the pier where Ron stood, apparently unconcerned about our leader's predicament, for despite Don's wearing his heavy mountain boots and being fully clothed, Ron's faith in him was resolute; they were both tough kids from Salford and had learned to swim in the Irwell.

Don surfaced, spitting and choking, his face twisted with temper.

"Me flat cap – where is it?" he shouted. It was, we observed, floating out into the middle of the loch, driven by the wind.

"Well," responded Cummaford calmly, as Whillans tried to tread water as

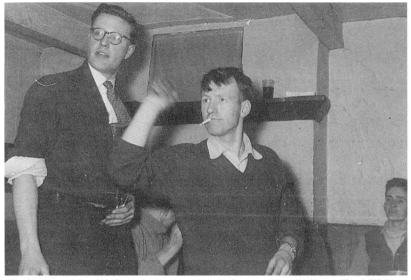

Alan Taylor and Don Whillans playing darts, Dennis Gray watching. Packhorse Hotel, Widdop, New Year's Eve 1960.   Photo: D G Verity

best as his Terray boots would allow, "is it salt water or fresh?"

"Fuck off ... Help me get out of here, yer bleeders!" which we then did by forming a human chain, each clinging to the pier, and holding out a tree branch lying conveniently at the landward end of the structure. (Perhaps that is what is was there for?) But I am still not sure if the water in Loch Etive is fresh or salt, for we never dared to mention the question to the Villain again.

That same night we visited the Kinghouse Hotel, situated on the edge of the Rannoch Moor, to meet friends from the Creag Dhu Club; John Cunningham, Bill Smith, Mick Noon and many others. We knew them from meetings in Wales and The Lakes, and both Whillans and I had climbed often enough with some of their number to become good friends. However, the evening was later to be disrupted against all of our wishes. Because of Don's reputation for aggression, he attracted would-be challengers – other hard men looking for a fight. This turned out to be one such occasion for one of the Dhus, a little the worse for drink, started trying to rile the Villain. But for once he was on his best behaviour and simply responded to the guy's oaths and threats with good-natured banter. This only seemed to enrage the Glaswegian the more.

"Dinna tak nae heed o' him, he's drunk!" advised Mick Noon, and we continued swapping stories about climbs and mutual friends.

Whillans, engaged in deep conversation with Cunningham and Smith, was standing in a corner with his back to Morty, Cummaford and me, who were equally involved, talking to Noon. But we were stopped in our round when the argumentative Glaswegian, a heavy, tough-looking man, suddenly reappeared and, producing an empty whisky bottle, calmly walked up behind the Villain, raised it and was about to smash it down on his head. I was frightened speechless, and neither Morty nor Ron moved a muscle – presumably they were also scared stiff as to what might happen next. But then, like a panther, Cunningham moved and, just as the guy was about to hit Don from behind, his hand was caught by his fellow Dhu in an arm lock.

"Drop it or I'll break yer arm."

"Aghh ... aghh!" the drunk shouted, and his arm flopped to his side. Cunningham let him go and he staggered out of the bar, not to be seen again that night. Later Cunningham came over to us and demanded, "Why did yer nae warn him? Why did yer nae tell Whillans the guy had a bottle in his haund?"

Ron looked at him for a moment and thoughtfully replied, "Because if he had hit Don he might have knocked him down, but he would have got back up off the floor and murdered the guy. He would never have lived to sneak up on anyone again ... the bloody coward!" Such was Cummaford's confidence in his fellow Salfordian. This really impressed the Dhus but not me, for if Cunningham had not intervened it might have been Don who had died from such a blow – I was under no illusions about Whillans' or anyone else's ability to take such a hit on the head with impunity.

Don did not always come out on top in such confrontations, and I do recall several occasions when he either took a beating or was saved from worse only by divine providence. But always the odds seemed stacked against him, and in this he was unique, for little appeared to intimidate him either in climbing situations or elsewhere. The most frightening escapade that I was involved in with him was on one winter's night in 1957, when we were camping in the woods at Stanage. (This was before the National Park had banned wild camping.) After climbing and cooking, Morty, Audrey, Don and I descended in my van to Hathersage to visit The Little John pub. When we arrived in The Little John, we found with some surprise that the public bar was enjoying a visit from the Sheffield Chapter of the Hell's Angels. About a dozen bikers were in the room, adorned in leather, swastikas and the rest of the paraphernalia, and the only place we could find to sit was at a table by the door. Every time this opened, a freezing, icy blast wafted over us. The Angels soon realised that the little guy sitting by the door was losing his cool, and that if they deliberately kept walking in and out, pretending to go to the bar or the toilet, they were really going to upset him. And so they did for all they were worth – in and out, in and out, and each time Don, who was on the outside of our table, had to get up to let them pass by. Soon rude comments were being exchanged, and bad language mouthed by the bikers, something to which Whillans took great exception in front of Audrey, his wife, who was trying to calm him down. Both Morty and I sat there, wondering if we might get out of the place alive.

The tension built up and up, but it was obvious to me that the bikers would not make the first move. We were too puny, too few to bother with, and if only Don had been prepared to back off and move to another pub, then all would have been well. But in 1957 that was not his style, and his anger was growing to the point where sooner or later the evening would erupt. I was wondering how we would make our escape – through a window, perhaps, or out the back door – when there was a knocking at the door above Don's head, and this time it was one of the Angels on a genuine mission. He had been to the bar and obtained a tray of drinks for his mates, and was using the edge of the tray to bang on the door to gain entry. At this Don slowly got to his feet and politely opened the door, but I caught sight of his face as he did this, and it was a mask of fury. The biker started through the opening, attempting to brush Don aside as he did so, and then, "Wham!" Whillans hit him with the door. The tray went flying and the biker went down. The next moment was pure theatre. Don whirled round, picking up his bar stool as he did so, and with this he rounded on the startled Hell's Angels. This took them by complete surprise, which was one of the Villain's most potent abilities in such circumstances, for few other climbers of my acquaintance would have gone on the attack as he did, actually herding the bikers into a defensive corner.

Morty and I were hiding under the table at this point and I heard Audrey saying, "Don, Don, don't hurt them..........!" from somewhere above our heads. Her faith in her consort was absolute, and in all truth she must have seen him do some amazing things over the years.

"You lot get outside ... get the van running!" Don commanded, whilst holding the Angels at bay with wild swipes of the bar stool. We needed no second bidding, and ran out into The Little John's yard, jumping over the sprawled figure in the passage. Before you could say "Stanage", I was into my Austin van, had the keys in the ignition and the engine running. Before you could say "The Unconquerables", the others piled in through the back door and, as we pulled out of the yard, Don came running and dived into the

passenger seat. I then drove up to the woods above North Lees farm below
Stanage as if the Hell's Angels were on my tail, which they were. We just
beat them to the finishing line, having better local knowledge. We then hid
the van down a small entry, quickly covering it with leaves and branches, and
sprinted down to our tents – Don and Audrey into his, Morty and I into
mine. All night long, on the lane above our heads we heard motor-bike
engines throbbing up and down, relentlessly searching for their prey. Morty
and I clung to each other, gripping our piton hammers and ready to put up a
struggle to save our skins, whilst from the tent next door came the sound of
snoring!

My own greatest climbing ambition in that era was to achieve a climb
called *Surplomb* on Clogwyn y Grochan in the Llanberis Pass. Those who
know this route and its history will know that it has suffered the fate of many
such extremes – it has gone from being the hardest problem in the Llanberis
Pass (at the time of its first ascent by Brown and Whillans in 1953) to one
accessible to a geriatric eccentric; therefore I ought really to try to repeat it. I
had made several unsuccessful attempts with Pat Walsh; on the first occasion
when he had lead up the initial wall, the most difficult section of the two-
pitch route, I had been unable even to second him. We had later returned
and I had led the crux of the wall without difficulty, only to fail as second on
the easier top chimney. Each occasion necessitated ignominious abseil
retreats for myself. Knowing my history, Whillans had decided to coach me
up this route, and one snowy day of the Easter holidays of 1958, after
reaching its base in a few minutes from the Grochan's field, I sat on the
scree holding his rope, explaining to Morty my problems over the last pitch.
"It's incredibly wide bridging up there. Walsh (who was also small like me,
but not as little as either Don or Morty) only just made it. And I couldn't
follow him because every time I tried to bridge out leftwards the rope was
pulling me off!"

"Yer a ninnie ....!" floated down from above our heads. "Watch me
bloody rope instead of gassing to Mortimer, yer little drink of water, its
greasy up here!"

"OK, Don!" I assured him, alarmed by the news that the rock was damp.
On looking up and taking an interest in our leader, as he had commanded, I
realised things were grim. Although I could see he was above the hardest
moves of the first pitch, the next section was causing him difficulties; he kept
slipping around on the wet rock and was obviously tiring badly. But then, in
typical Whillans' fashion, he did something revolutionary – the very first time
I ever saw this feat performed on a rock-face. He made a figure of four out of

Don Whillans (Ian Howell in the background) on Gauri Sankar, 1964. Photo: D Gray

Don Whillans leading *Surplomb*, 1958.
Photo: Mrs Audrey Whillans

his body, got his right hand on a good spike, brought his leg high and over this and then sat and rested on his hand, still holding onto the rock but beneath his trunk. I am assured by those who can repeat this feat that it is a good way to get a breather. Recently I have seen in French climbing magazines (circa 1990) how they have invented this important new climbing technique, especially in order to climb smooth, extreme routes like Chouca at Buoux .... mais, mes amis, le Villain – il utilisait cette technique en 1958! He confessed afterwards to having seen a gymnast do this in his youth, but I would hazard a guess that this was one of the first occasions it was used in a climbing situation.

Eventually Don reached the belay at the top of the first pitch and, with much swearing and grunting from us, brought first Morty and then me up to his perch. It was obvious when I arrived that Don was expecting me to lead the next pitch, but my previous failed attempts had totally undermined me. As soon as I set forth and had bridged up a few feet, I scuttled back down to the safety of the good ledge on which Morty sat holding my rope. The top pitch of *Surplomb* begins with a 20 foot narrow, slippy, black chimney that disappears in a roof (set about 100 feet above the ground and, in those days before nuts, totally unprotectable). At the roof, the only obvious exit is to swing left in order to gain a crack and the easier finishing wall, a manoeuvre that was – Whillans kept assuring me – both easy and well-supplied with holds. My attempts became more determined and I actually did get to the top of the chimney, but could not reach any of those so-called good holds, and in extremis retreated just before I fell off.

"Bloody hell, Slippery Jim" (this nickname, I think, awarded to me by Don as a result of a battle on the Grochan's field – the Apprentices versus the Master – when we nearly killed Joe), "yer can bridge up and down this bleeding thing all day. Watch me.........!" and not waiting to see if we had hold of his rope, a bored Whillans proceeded to do just that, up and down, bridging easily up to the top of the chimney, until he reached a good hand-hold out on the left, then back down again – only facing outwards! He made it look so easy that after he had demonstrated this method a couple of times, I decided to try it. But I could not even get into the same position as he had been in and, ashamedly, I had to ask Morty to have a go, for my legs were by then shaking like a sewing machine from the efforts I had been making.

Morty, facing in, and with a more traditional style, then managed to climb it for, although he was smaller and younger than I was, he was much stronger and a better climber. Then, with Don urging me on from below, cheering my every move, I finally managed to get up the bloody thing. Whillans could be frightening on the ground, but on a crag, especially with Morty and me, he encouraged us, and I used to enjoy climbing with him then just because of that. We were privileged to have his example, and it was almost as if a group of kids from Leeds 6 were being coached by Boycott – or perhaps not quite!

Shortly after this event we held a Rock and Ice meet at my parents' home and, to my astonishment, my father took to Whillans like a soul mate. From thereon until his death in 1972 my Dad enjoyed frequent visits from Don, and occasionally took him on club dates. By that time my father was the epitome of the northern stand-up comedian and entertainer, and I believe that some of Don's later ability at 'one-liners' and repartee owes its origin to mixing in those circles. Initially his wit was more caustic than funny, but slowly over the years it softened and became more apposite and humane, and therefore more universal and humorous.

On the weekend of that meet we climbed at Almscliff and, but for Eric 'Matey' Metcalf suffering a fall, *The Wall of Horrors* might have received its first ascent from Brown and Whillans, three years before Allan Austin completed his epic first ascent. Joe had climbed the first difficult section up to the first horizontal break, and was fiddling around trying to fix a

After the first British ascent of the *Walker Spur*, Grandes Jorasses. L to R: Don Whillans, Les Brown, Robin Smith, Gunn Clark, and John Streetly in Courmayeur.   Photo: H MacInnes

chockstone in the crack, with rocks being thrown up to him by Don, Eric Price and myself. But we had to abandon these activities when Matey fell. He was climbing with Morty on the *Northwest Girdle* and fell, hitting the ground, whilst crossing the *Central Climb*. Happily, although we had to carry him down and Joe, Morty and I took him unconscious to Harrogate hospital, he quickly recovered and was allowed to leave that same night with us. I, however, was not so lucky when Morty, who had no idea of his true strength, decided to give me an extra warm greeting for some reason, and pulled at my right arm, dislocating it from its socket! I wandered around for a week like that, until the following weekend, when I passed out as Morty jumped on me when I was lying in the back of my van, unable to get out of my sleeping bag because of my injury. I subsequently had to have it put back, under anaesthetic at Leeds General Infirmary.

In the summer of 1958 I was in Chamonix with Whillans, Brown and Morty and, after tossing a coin for it, it was decided that I would climb with the Villain and Morty with the Baron Brown. I had previously climbed in the Eastern Alps but never in the Mont Blanc range – in other words I was a novice. This mattered not one whit to Don, and with him I made an early ascent of the East Face of the Grand Capucin. During the descent we got caught in a real humdinger of a storm, against which our protection was a large, heavy-gauge polythene bag, normally used for covering paper-stacks in a printing works. I had brought this out from England with me, and once the blizzard set in we spent many hours sitting inside that impermeable fabric, balanced on a tiny ledge on the side of Mont Blanc du Tacul, with a primus stove roaring in between us and Don chain-smoking Gaulois. My lungs almost collapsed with the fug, but the Villain seemed impervious in those days to such considerations.

During that season we spent a lot of time with a group of Austrian climbers at the Chalet Austria, a wood-cutters' shelter near Montenvers above the Mer de Glace. Amongst the Austrians were Walter Phillip, Dieter Marchart (later to perish in a solo attempt on the North Face of the Eiger) and the youthful Richard Blach. We spent much of our daylight hours either working at climbing problems on the walls of the hut, or brewing the inevitable tea – the Austrians declared that they had never seen anyone drink so much of the amber liquid! Our companions were not only good company but, like ourselves, young, impecunious and dedicated to climbing.

It has been written about Whillans that no man carved his personality out of the rock-face more than he did. Many of the routes he pioneered were fierce and uncompromising for the era before modern protection techniques – climbs like *Extol* on Dove Crag in the Lake District, *Erosion Groove Direct* on Carreg Wastad in the Llanberis Pass, *Taurus* on Cloggy or *Goliath* at Burbage Edge in Derbyshire. On these first ascents, like Brown, he only rarely seemed to struggle, and one wonders what he might have achieved with modern equipment such as sticky-soled boots, better ropes and protection devices like 'Friends' and 'Rocks'. Don turned away from British rock-climbing in the early 1960s, when he must have been as good as anybody then active on that scene, and before the introduction of such modern equipment; he went on to concentrate on Alpinism and, thereafter, the Himalaya, for which his best climbing performances were reserved. I firmly believe that some of the leads he made on the Gauri Sankar expedition of 1964 are as hard technically as any yet made at altitude – rock-climbing of Va/Vb and high-standard snow and ice-climbing.

Few, if any, of his new routes were pioneered during the nut protection era, and the very first time I remember seeing anybody using these on a climb, Don was there and took exception. This was sometime in the mid-50s and we had walked up to Clogwyn y Grochan to climb *Slape Direct*. As we passed the groove of *Brant* we caught sight of a climber, bridged high up this route but with a huge machine nut on a sling, which he was trying to throw into the crack above his head.

"Oi, mate, Whitworth! If yer can't climb the routes as they were first done, then pack it in!" Don shouted up angrily at the hapless leader, as we shuffled past to reach the foot of our adjacent route. The poor chap seemed so undermined by being told off by Whillans that he retreated, but we were surprised when he did reach the ground to see that he had several slings around his neck, and that on each one was a machine nut.

"Eh, Whitworth, whose motorbike did yer get them off?" demanded the Villain, probably worried that it might be his own. The climber was so embarrassed by these strictures that he promptly packed up and disappeared down the scree slope, never to be seen again. Later, Whillans recalled him by his nickname, always citing his behaviour as climbing trickery and cheating! I often think of 'Whitworth' when I read in climbing histories of how so-and-so introduced nuts into Lakeland climbing, or that so-and-so did the same in Wales, or even that Jack Soper invented the famous wired, wedge-shaped nut in the 1960s. Poor old 'Whitworth' was years ahead of them all, and if Whillans had still been pioneering when Soper, Crew, Ingle, Boysen et al started using nuts for protection in the early 1960s, they too might have been subjected to the same verbal abuse. But as for doing the routes as he climbed them originally, – few of us could have done.

Over the years, I was privileged to watch Don pioneer some of his own routes, including the fierce *Cave Wall* at Froggat Edge in 1958, but the most impressive piece of rock-climbing I saw him do in Britain was at Black Rocks in the winter of 1959. This was the first occasion on which most of the group had been to Cromford and, under Nat Allen's guidance, who, living in Derby, was one of the local experts, we camped in the wood on the steep slopes at the western side of the outcrop. We then set about repeating the great classics of the edge with gusto: Steve Read and I climbed the *Promontory Traverse,* then the *Superstitious Start* and the *Lean Man's Super Direct,* but after this we stuck on *Demon Rib,* Harding's difficult route from the 1940s, the gymnastic moves necessary to get off the ground turning us back. Pat Walsh appeared and, donning his PAs, flowed up these by bringing his feet up to his hands, and then reaching high with his left hand whilst holding his weight on his right. By this method he reached a small hold, stood up, and then proceeded by a series of thin laybacks to gain the final moves of the climb, where he stuck, obviously in some difficulty. But after several anxious moments, at a mantelshelf 25 feet up, he finally made the pull over to reach a good ledge on his right, and finished easily up the arête above this to reach the top of the crag. He shouted laughingly down to us, "Aye, it's a hard wee problem, boys! It would'nae be out o' place on the Whangie!" This was the ultimate in Scottish denigration, for the Whangie was trotted out by Pat whenever he wished to deflate the English egos: those who know the place would admit it is hardly Slime Wall, being more akin to Harborough Rocks!

Whillans had observed this action from the slope at our side, huddled in his duvet and wearing a pair of mountain boots recently made to measure by an Austrian bootmaker. They looked like pit boots and they certainly were heavy, but none of us dared say so – he was very proud of them, claiming that they were a breakthrough in winter climbing footwear. (This was, of course, before double boots were developed in 1961.)

At Pat's performance, and subsequent comment, he wandered over to the foot of Demon Rib, stripped off his duvet and started playing around on the first holds.

"This is how you do it, Slippery Jim. Right hand on the little jug, feet up to your hands, then hold yourself, then reach high with your left hand into that little groove up on the left. Small crimp hold there, just enough to hold yer while yer get the layback and away yer go!"

And we were astonished as he set off up after Pat, placing his boots carefully on little rugosities, climbing smoothly and quickly up what had been considered one of the hardest outcrop leads of the previous generation. He had no trouble until he reached the top of the rib but then, like Pat, stuck at the final moves.

"Are you OK, Don?"

"Yer..........," and then he almost jumped into the mantelshelf, swinging out to his right to finish by sitting on his right hand as if he was resting. He maintained this position for a long time before bringing his clumsy boots up and standing high on his left foot, balanced up on this, then climbed easily up the final rib and grabbed the top with his hands; and with a last leap up-and-over the skyline, he was there! Despite this example, it was to be many dozens of attempts and two years later before I managed to climb *Demon Rib*. But I was wearing PAs, not heavy mountain boots, and could not have made it in such footgear.

I have read recently that EBs were the first and original specialist rock-climbing boot, but this is not so. The confusion has arisen because the first such boot design, developed by Pierre Allain for bouldering at Fontaine-bleau in 1948, was sold in the 1960s to Emile Bourdenau, and from then on became known as EBs. For a decade before this they were universally known

Harry Smith on *The Cardinal*, Earl Sterndale.   Photo: D Gray

as PAs. To further complicate the matter, having sold out, Pierre Allain then introduced another boot design onto the market as PAs, but nothing could compare at that time with the original. They first appeared in the UK in the early 1950s, and I managed to obtain a pair in the summer of 1954, when Joe Brown brought me a pair back from Chamonix. Until that period all hard climbs in Britain were usually led in gym pumps!

Another Rock and Ice climber of the early 1960s who could climb the hardest routes in boots was Harry Smith. He joined the club when it was re-formed by Nat Allen and myself in 1959 (after its disbandment in 1958), and he remains one of the least known but strongest rock-climbers in my experience. Harry was a wonderful eccentric, who looked almost like an escapee from a 'Three Stooges' film, with a long, lean, powerful body, angular face, and wispy hair growing out from a semi-bald head at acute angles. He was a plasterer and, due to financial stringencies, he nearly always climbed in knackered footgear: old boots or other climbers' cast-offs. He spoke with a high-pitched Brum accent, and he and Whillans, who were almost contemporaries, were like a comedy duo when climbing together.

In 1960 Don was away on Trivor in the Himalaya, and afterwards drove back from Rawalpindi to Rawtentstall on a Triumph motor-cycle: an amazing journey, during which he was attacked by Pathans on the Khyber

Pass, had run-ins with the frontier guards in Yugoslavia and was shot at by customs officials in Bulgaria. He arrived back in November, when we met up in North Wales and travelled in my van from Llanberis to Tremadog, where we had agreed to meet Harry Smith. Earlier that year Joe Brown had pioneered some important new routes there, including *Vector* and *The Slip* routes, which were being lauded for their difficulty by the North Wales regulars, and we decided we ought to take a look at them. We met up with Harry (whom we knew as The Kid) when we arrived at the crag. He was seething with anger at Whillans, for he had just heard that he had been impugned in a book to be published about the Trivor expedition. Wilf Noyce, the author, had written about an incident when climbing with Don on Cloggy: there had been a loud commotion – shouting, swearing and screams from another part of the cliff. Anxiously, Wilf had enquired of his leader, who was bridged out above his head whilst making the first ascent of a Direct Finish to *The Sheaf* climb, "What is it? What's happening?" to be reassured by the laconic response, "It's only Harry falling off again!"

"I've never fallen off in me life. I'll sue, I'll sue ... It's a downright lie!" was Harry's greeting when we met him at the base of Vector Buttress on Bwlch y Moch.

"Oh, shut it ...... Let's have a look at these routes that Curly Legs" (one of our nicknames for Brown) "has put out."

Whillans insisted that he was unfit after motor-cycling the 7000 miles from Pakistan, and so I was thrust into the lead up the easy first pitch of *Vector*. Then, hanging off a pinnacle belay, I brought Harry up and he led up to the first crux of the climb, the Ochre Slab. He climbed onto this and, after some teetering about, he managed to ascend it, then traversed left to reach a cave and piton belays at the end of this now famous key pitch. I brought Don up and, with great difficulty, fought my way up the Ochre Slab to reach Harry, to be joined by the Villain seconds later for, despite his protestations about his fitness, he had arrived back lean and still strong. We had no description as to where we should go from the cave, but had heard it said that you climbed out leftwards, over a roof, down a slab, then up a crack.

"I'll lead the top pitch. It looks bloody interesting!" Don decided, and in all truth we were full of admiration for the Baron's new climb. Harry was entertaining us with stories of the epics Joe had enjoyed in doing this, and graphically told of how his would-be seconds kept parting company with the rock-face, and then needed to be lowered back to the ground, unable to get back into contact with the route.

"They say it was like Joe Brown's flying circus ...," he commented. Harry

Dennis Gray leading *Vector*.   Photo: Gray coll.

could be very funny when he was in the story-telling mood, and we were so
engaged by his descriptions that we had not noticed that the weather was
deteriorating rapidly and rain clouds were sweeping in from Portmadog Bay.

"Bloody hell!" we heard from Don out to the left of us, "It's starting to
rain." He had climbed out of the cave, over the roof and, after descending
down a slab, now stood beneath the difficult final crack. 'Woosh!' down it
came – within minutes it was pouring down with large raindrops.

"Watch me rope, I'm coming back!" and as Harry took in his rope, we saw
his figure reappear to our left. Moments later he was back in the cave
alongside The Kid and myself.

"Hey, what are you doing?" demanded Harry as Don tied himself in with
a sling, but then untied off the rope and started threading it through an in
situ piton.

"Me? I'm going down. You can stay here if you like," and as soon as he
had a rope set up, he was sliding down it in a sit-sling abseil. We had no
alternative but to follow, for we knew that once the Villain had made up his
mind it was final; and thus *Vector* had to wait some time longer for its second
ascent – other than by Brown, who repeated his creation – by which date it
had gained an incredible reputation for difficulty with so many would-be
leaders falling off.

There was a sequel to Harry's objections about Don's comment as to his 'always falling off', published in the Trivor book. The following summer he found himself at the foot of Tremadog once again, a week or so after Brown had pioneered a route he had called *The Grasper*. He had persuaded Whillans to accompany him to attempt the second ascent; already by that date Don was beginning to take a lower profile on the British cliffs and was therefore willing to follow The Kid up the whole of the route, on the safe end of the rope. *The Grasper* has two pitches: a slabby start leads to an awkward roof which, when overcome, gives way to a steep wall and a small nook with almost a hanging belay from a spike; followed by a second pitch up a hanging groove set on the steepest wall of Craig Bwlch y Moch. To climb this groove on the first ascent, Joe had used two pitons – one low down and then a second to exit from the top of the feature, where it was capped by a roof. All went well with the Smith/Whillans attempt until Harry reached the final moves of the climb, where he had to make an exit out of the groove, fifty feet above Don's head.

He put a sling into the piton left in place by Joe, which, typical of Brown, was in to the hilt, right in the best position. Harry stood up in this and was just about to reach the big jug hold with his hands when there was a 'ping' and the piton shot out of the crack. "Ch...r...i...s...t!" and Harry was hurtling down the cliff. The next second the pull came on Whillans, hanging on the spike, smoking a fag and contemplating the infinity of the skyline.

"Bloody hell!" The force of it pulled him upside down, but he held onto Harry's rope, which was of overweight nylon. Thankfully, the second peg in the groove held, but Harry finished many feet below The Villain, looking up at him swinging backwards and forwards off the spike. Don had lost his flat cap, his fags, and his hands were burned, but on this occasion he said nothing as Harry got back onto the rock, and he pulled himself upright once more.

"That bugger Brown! I'll tell him something when I meet him ... He doesn't know how to put peetons in!" The Kid was saying as he climbed back up past Whillans, then proceeded to ascend the groove once more, and again all went well until the final moves, set high above Whillans' perch.

"I'll put me own pegs in in future!" Harry was saying as he hammered home a channel piton to the hilt. He put a sling on this, stood up in it and then was reaching for the final holds high up on the left – but just as he was about to announce that he was up, 'ping!' out shot the peg and he took his second swallow-dive down the cliff.

"Oh, no ......!" shouted Whillans as, once again, he was dragged off his perch to suffer rope burns for a second time. The Kid found himself swinging once more beneath an upside-down Whillans and now the object of his wrath.

"I was bleeding right," he decided, "you're always falling off!" as he lowered poor Harry safely back down to the ground.

It is interesting to note that, as Don began to lose interest in his major pioneering activities in Britain, he became keener on gritstone 'bouldering'. By 1960 he and Audrey were living in a cottage at Crawshaw Booth in the Rossendale Valley (they had married in 1957), and in the winter months over the next few years he would spend his weekends on the boulders at Widdop, the nearby Bridestones, or in trips down to Stanage, where he would boulder for hours playing around on the outcrops in the plantation. A new generation has now found the worth of these activities, but I wonder if any of them have yet found 'The King Swing' at this latter venue? This entailed climbing a high tree and leaping out of it to catch a rope fastened to a branch of an adjacent trunk, then to hurtle through space and, at the end of its trajectory, leap onto a boulder with a terrible landing at its foot, and then ascend it. I never dared to do this myself, but saw The Villain manage it several times.

On one such occasion in 1960 I had arranged to meet Don in Hathersage to spend a Saturday afternoon 'bouldering' up at Stanage. I waited at the appointed place outside the Ordnance Arms, but he did not turn up by the agreed hour, which was very unusual, for he was always a stickler for punctuality. I waited for him a long time, thinking that he might have had an accident or a breakdown travelling down from Lancashire on his bike. Just as I was about to depart, he arrived, with his head swathed in bandages under his flat cap.

"What happened to you? Did you come off the bike?" I gasped at the sight of him.

"No. Never try to help anybody else .... I learnt my bloody lesson this morning, mate!" Don responded.

"How come, what happened?" I enquired, guessing that he might have been in some kind of physical misunderstanding with superior forces yet again.

"I went into work," (he was still working as a plumber then) "and as I was crossing the building site I saw this Irish labourer struggling along, pushing a barrow with a heavy load of pipes. So I went over to give him a hand in shoving it, and as we passed under one of the buildings we were working on, a stupid bleeder dropped a scaffolding pole on our heads. Fortunately the Irishman was bigger than me, and it hit him first and then bounced onto my head."

"Bloody hell, how is he?" I ventured to enquire.

"He's unconscious in hospital with a badly fractured skull, poor bugger."

"How about you? What's the damage?" I asked,

"Ten bleeding stitches, mate, and a hairline fracture of the skull. My head aches like it's going to bust. Yer know, Slippery Jim, I'm going to stop being so helpful to people in future. I've learned me lesson," The Villain decided. I did not dare suggest that I had not really noticed his altruism in this respect in the past, and decided that the best policy was sympathy with his views.

"I don't blame you," I agreed.

"Do yer know, there's a very funny side to this happening? It's almost as if I'm being warned by the fates, not to be so willing about helping people in the future," he went on, and I have to admit that when he was in that philosophical mood of his, he could be very profound, and unconsciously funny.

"Six months ago, this same Irishman was working on another building site which I was at, and he was struggling with a barrow-load of bricks. So I dropped me bag and went to help him push it, but as we passed by under the house we working on, some daft bugger dropped a tile from up on the roof, and it hit him on the head, badly fracturing his skull and then bouncing off to cut me. The poor bleeder had only just come back to work this week after six months off due to that last fractured skull. I tell you, Slippery Jim, somebody up there (he jerked his thumb up in the air) is trying to tell me something!"

"Bloody hell, Don, it sounds like where you work is more dangerous than the Eiger for falling objects?" I admitted.

"Yes, yer can say that again. But it's cured me. NNext time I see some bugger needing a push I'll just go off round the next corner and mind me own business. I've got to rid myself of me natural feelings of generosity. By the way, the pubs are open and it's your round!"

And as I got in the first pints (the first of many) I had to accept that there were some grounds for the logic in The Villain's philosophy, which only seemed to underline his long-held belief that life was a constant battle against incredible chicanery, hostile forces and a black fate which were all conspiring to bring him down. Standing at the bar in the Ordnance Arms, his head bandaged like a First World War veteran, a pint in his hand, a fag in the corner of his mouth, he went on to observe thoughtfully, as he took his first drink of the day, "It's a bloody hard life, Slippery Jim – if yer don't weaken!"

"What happens if you do, Don?" I cautiously enquired.

"Yer get a bleeding great blow on yer head, mate, that's what!" And in view of his physical condition there was no arguing with that statement, which I guessed was final.

At Don's suggestion we had a Rock and Ice meet at Widdop Rocks for the New Year celebrations of 1960, staying in a huge barn at the side of the nearby Packhorse Pub. There was deep snow on the ground as a large contingent of us, including Nat Allen and his wife Tinsel, Morty Smith, Eric Beard, many more of the group and non-club members, such as the youthful Martin Boysen, assembled at the rocks for a day's 'bouldering' in heavy boots, before repairing back to our quarters to cook. We dubbed the barn 'Dracula's' for it was then an evil place: damp, dark, and with the biggest cobwebs I have even seen. We then entered the hostelry to begin our New Year's Eve celebrations, but these were soon interrupted by the arrival of a contingent of the Manchester Gritstone Club, led by the late Barry Kershaw, who had a similar reputation to Whillans for aggressive behaviour. In later years Barry, who was bigger and darker in looks than Don, became his close friend but, at this first real meeting, it was not long before he and The Villain were squaring up to each other. A challenge was thrown down at darts – our Rock and Ice arrows team was led by Eric Beard (who had once been in the last sixteen of the *News of the World* championships), supported by Doug Verity, who was also good at the game, and had Whillans as their third team member. (He was incredibly keen on the game, but never in their class.) By the light of oil lamps and flickering candles to illuminate the board, we thrashed the Grits. This then led to a physical contest, and the bar was cleared and teams picked for competitions in press-ups, pull-ups on a beam and arm wrestling. This latter went to a final between Whillans and Kershaw, and the atmosphere was electric. It was like a scene from a Hollywood movie as the two hard men locked fists across a bar table, whilst their supporters cheered them on.

Suddenly, both participants lost their tempers and, forgetting about the rules and the table, were arm wrestling around the room, knocking aside us spectators like skittles. First Barry got the upper hand and then Don, and it was obvious that, at any moment, they would forget about arm wrestling and be fighting for real. At this point the barman, who had up until that moment been leaning against his counter and obviously enjoying our antics, decided that enough was enough, for tables were being knocked over and glasses broken.

"Alright, boys that's it, cut it out!" he commanded, but Whillans and Kershaw took not a blind bit of notice and continued pushing each other around the room.

"I said that's enough!" the barman reiterated, with exactly the same effect – the two combatants kept on at each other, snarling and threatening, pulling and pushing.

"Right, yer buggers, you've asked for it!" and, to our astonishment, the barman vaulted the bar and made for the fray. We were surprised at both his agility and his size, for he was by far the biggest guy in the room; what we had not realised was that there was a gutter down behind the bar, which had hidden most of his height from us. He grabbed Whillans and Kershaw, separating them as if they were children and easily holding them by either hand at arm's length.

"Now boys, if you're going to play, then do it properly, or I'll knock your bloody heads together. You've broken some glasses, and either you pay for them or you're out through the door – understood?" Both Don and Barry were taken off balance by this sudden attack from the side, but it certainly calmed them down, for they were now looking up into the face of a much superior force.

"OK! OK!" they both agreed.

"I'll tell you what, lads, I'll give you a go at arm wrestling!" the barman offered, but Don took one look at him and declined, being for once totally outfaced. We learned later, on subsequent visits, that the barman, who was actually the landlord, was a professional wrestler – 'The Blond Strangler'. During further visits he became as keen on the Rock and Ice game sessions as we were, and he eventually mastered Morty's trick of being able to stand up from lying face down with someone sitting on his shoulders. Thankfully, he was not a climber!

Don and Audrey's cottage in Crawshaw Booth was a well-placed haven. Don had been evacuated to the village towards the end of the last war, and since had always wanted to return to escape the grime and smoke of Salford. Audrey is one of the warmest and kindest women I have met. A mountaineer herself (she has climbed in the Himalaya), she was almost saint-like in her understanding and kindness towards us, and in putting up with Don's waywardness and climbing ambitions, which meant that for most of their life together his interest lay in the world of mountains and did not lead him into developing a business or settling down to a steady working routine in life.

We had several weekends staying at their home in the winter months in the early 1960s, 'bouldering' at the Bridestones, a small gritstone escarpment straddling an exposed ridge in the Pennines, and consisting of a long jumble of boulders which are known locally as 'The Kebs' because of their unusual rounded shapes. I did once manage to repeat one of Don's hardest problems there on a visit from Derby with Nat Allen in the winter of 1962. This was the infamous *Duck* – a very hard jamming-crack that really made you quack! However, his hardest problem there, *The Villain*, nobody else could climb, and I believe that it was almost a decade before it was repeated. Whillans was so proud of this that he actually offered to buy a pint for any other climber who could get up it. But none of us could.

By June 1964 our plans for the expedition on Gauri Sankar in the Rolwaling Himalaya were completed. The night before we were due to leave, we had an all-night party at Crawshaw Booth. Don had persuaded a local brewery to donate two 216-pint barrels of beer for this event, delivering them to his local pub. Ian Howell and myself were delayed by the manufacturer making last-minute adjustments and preparations to the Landrover in which five of us were to set off next morning to drive to Kathmandu. By the time we arrived it was closing time but we found, of course, that the huge barrels would not go into the body of the vehicle. Thus, everybody in the pub that night joined forces to roll them up the hill to Whillans' house. With the arrival a short while later of Tom Patey (who had driven from Ullapool) and his accordian, a ceilidh was soon under way.

Our fun was interrupted in the early hours of the morning by the dramatic arrival into our midst of a well-preserved, petite, dark-haired and good-looking woman. She burst dramatically into the room and walked up to Don who, a little the worse for drink, was engaged in some tomfoolery with the rest of the party-goers, trying to balance a drink on his forehead. Halting in front of him, her next actions were amazing.

"Don't think I'm frightened of you, Don Whillans," she screamed out, and 'Wham!' she hit him right between the eyes with an uppercut that would have done justice to a Lonsdale belt holder. Don staggered and went down. I had been accompanying Patey, plonking away on my tenor banjo, but my fingers fell idle at such an extraordinary turn. Tom also stopped playing abruptly.

"Bloody hell! Who is she?" he demanded.

"It could be one of those new liberated women from the Pinnacle Club?" I surmised.

Everybody else was amazed, and even Don seemed dumbstruck, but once back up on his feet he stared at his attacker through an alcoholic haze, sizing up the opposition, obviously trying to decide what it was that had hit him so hard. Then he exploded, and before anyone could restrain him he leapt at the woman and shouted, "And don't think I wouldn't hit a woman, 'cos I would!" and he landed a blow onto the woman's chest that sent her sprawling across the room.

"Jesus ......!" I heard Patey gasp, and then everybody joined in – half a dozen people grabbing Whillans, and even more pairs of hands taking hold of the lady, who had scattered several bodies as she shot across the room.

"Yer a rotten bugger!" she decided, picking herself up with a dozen pairs of arms restraining her.

"If yer don't get out of my house, I'll kill yer," responded Don, pulling hard against his own holders. At this juncture the door opened and in walked a tall, well-dressed gentleman, wearing a raincoat and a Homburg hat.

"Come on Violet, that's enough!" he commanded and, linking his arm in hers and doffing his hat to us, he proceeded to frog-march her out through the door, still kicking and struggling as she went.

"Who the hell was she?" I demanded of Don, once things had calmed down.

"Just one of the locals. They're me biggest fans, yer know," he informed me with some pride.

"Bloody hell, Tom, let's get this ceilidh going again," I pleaded with Patey. Hours later, still playing, we greeted the daylight as it came filtering through Don's front room window, and I realised that it would soon be time to hit the road to Kathmandu.

Six weeks later Ian Clough, Terry Burnell, Ian Howell and myself reached that city, having left behind Dez Hadlum at Raxaul on the Indian border with Nepal to await The Villain's arrival with our two tons of equipment and food. Don had accompanied our gear by sea from Liverpool to Bombay and then overland across India. This may sound a simple procedure, but those who have never done it cannot imagine the frustration, exacerbated by the heat, of bureaucratic delay. It was my turn to act as equipment nursemaid after the expedition, and just traversing Benares, changing stations with three four-hundredweight boxes, carried by eight coolies per crate was a major undertaking. By the time Whillans arrived at the Nepalese border after many days of coping with the Bombay bureaucrats, train guards and transport officials, he was on a short fuse. I expected that we might have some kind of trouble when he arrived at the notorious customs post at Raxaul to try to gain entry to Nepal. I was not proved wrong. We had brought our two tons of equipment in wooden shipping crates, and on arrival at Raxaul by lorry, the chief customs officer insisted that they be off-loaded by Whillans and Dez, and that the lids come off in order for him to compare the contents with the lists we had prepared of the goods we were bringing into

Nepal. This took more than a day to do, but after much work by Don and his partner it was at last completed, the boxes were resealed and, with a lot of heaving, pushing and lifting in the withering heat of a hot, tropical sun, all was ready: the vehicle, The Villain, Dez and the equipment, safely fastened down to set out for Kathmandu.

Just as they were leaving, a clerk came running out of the office and announced, "All procedures have not been properly completed! Could you please unload your boxes again, Mr Whillans?" At this, Don lost his temper and marched back into the office to give the chief customs officer a piece of his mind.

"You can lift those bleeding boxes off yerself, mate," he told him. "Yer a bleeding waste of time!" This led on to verbal abuse from the chief of customs as to the nature of Don's parentage, and when The Villain gave him an equal amount of chat in reply, the chief summoned an armed guard. Up to this point Dez – the most gentle of souls – had been a spectator, but when he tried to take a placatory role received a shove that flung him across the room. This was too much for Don to bear and 'Wham!' he retaliated, at which the whole scene erupted into a free-for-all. The resulting mêlée was broken up by the arrival of a squad of Ghurkas. And the rest, as they say, is history. It took a round of urgent late-night meetings in Kathmandu, plus the intervention of our Ambassador, aided by the Military Attaché, Charles Wylie (fortunately himself a mountaineer) to sort out the row. Finally their combined efforts kept Dez and Don from the threatened jail sentence.

The outcome of the Gauri Sankar expedition was a terrible disappointment to our mainly Rock and Ice Club team (four of the party of six were club members), for Don and Ian Clough only just failed to climb the mountain's incredibly difficult north face. But even at the time, Whillans was philosophic in defeat: "You win some, you lose some," was very much his attitude. He was always very sane about risk-taking in the mountains. He and Ian Clough turned back due to avalanche risk, when only a few hundred feet of ascent would have meant reaching the summit. I have recently read criticisms of Don's success rate in the Himalaya, and it is true that he failed on his various expeditions to reach the top in more cases than not. But when I consider now how many other good friends died there subsequently, I cannot but feel that Don's judgement in these matters was superior.

"Yer picked a good 'un that time, Slippery Jim," he advised me as we bouldered around in the snow at Widdop on the weekend of my return at the end of the following January.

"What do yer think we should try next?" he asked, obviously meaning another Rock and Ice Club expedition.

"The South Face of Annapurna. I've already asked Jimmy Roberts in Kathmandu to try to get us permission," I laughingly suggested. Don was immediately enthusiastic, but it was not to be, for although we then started planning, picked a team, mainly made up of the Gauri Sankar party, and began making preparations, Nepal closed its borders to climbers later that year, and that was the end of my own involvement with the project. Eventually I passed it on to Chris Bonington. When, in 1970, that country did re-open its borders to mountaineers, Whillans and Dougal Haston were successful in climbing this futuristic objective. But Ian Clough, our other star from the Gauri Sankar expedition, was killed at the very end of the expedition. As a close friend from his earliest climbing days at Ilkley, I am forced to observe that it was a terrible price to pay for success.

The early 1970s were to be Whillans' golden Himalayan period: there was the success of the Annapurna climb, his career zenith; and several attempts on the South-West Face of Everest, during which he reached the highest point then attained. He became something of a celebrity, but was unchanged by this, and remained the outstanding example in the climbing world of the anti-hero – a bit Chaplinesque, the little man with a hat, except that Don's was a flat cap. His lecturing skills developed and, though he did appeal to a wide audience, he was at his best talking to climbers, when he was peerless in making them laugh and in taking them along with him, winning them over to an evening of enjoyment – the Don Whillans way.

Bob Pettigrew tells a story about one such lecture that he organised. On the way to the venue in Darlington, they could not get near the hall for a traffic jam. Eventually, Whillans climbed out of the vehicle and went up to a policeman who was directing the traffic, to try to find out what the hold up was about.

"What's up, mate, is there a football match on or something?" he demanded. "No, it's some climber they're all going to hear lecture at the Polytechnic. Beats me why anyone should want to go to listen to some boring bloke talking for hours on end," the copper confided.

"Yer, they'd be better off sitting in the pub with a pint in their hands," agreed Don.

By the mid-1970s, both Brown and Whillans had become national climbing institutions, a natural outcome of which in Britain is that you are liable to get an honour bestowed upon you by the Queen. As I was the General Secretary of the BMC, with the support of the Executive Committee we put their names forward on behalf of the Council, to be

Don Whillans being interviewed after winning the Miss Buxton Conference Competition 1984. Interviewer: "And what do you want to be when you grow up?" Whillans: "A short, fat, hairy climber."

considered for an honour for their example and contribution to mountaineering. This was, of course, done without their knowledge, and I was a little worried that Don might not be too pleased. I need not have worried for, typically, just as it was going through the official channels, and receiving universal support, The Villain was involved in one of the biggest punch-ups of his life – near to his home in Crawshaw Booth. Was it simply a case of old habits ? I now wonder.

It involved several policeman a damaged police car, and the newspaper reports the morning after the incident were lurid, to say the least. "He was like a wild animal!" one police sergeant was reported as saying. Another declared, "It was like fighting ten men!" and the tabloids had a field day with their headlines: "Everest climber in jail!" they reported.

The first I knew about it was when one of the Rock and Ice phoned the morning after to say that Don was in trouble and was being held in the nick. He was let out later the same day. It all began with Don being stopped whilst driving home from the pub and a policeman being rather officious with him. This had developed into a real slanging match, and unfortunately Don had then lashed out. Things got totally out of control after this event, for reserves were summoned and a battle developed between The Villain and five officers, who eventually subdued him; but not before he had damaged a panda car.

It was heartening to see how all Don's friends rallied round, but it was a case of limiting the damage, for there was no excusing his behaviour. My own contribution was to write a letter to the Court when the case came up before the bench. Using BMC notepaper, I declared that he was a great mountaineer and that he was held in the highest esteem by our fraternity. He was fined a large sum of money, banned from driving for a good spell, and bound over to be on his best behaviour in future. At the height of all this scandal I was phoned by the Prime Minister's office and the conversation ran roughly along the following lines:

"Mr Gray?"

"Er, yes?"

"This Mr Don Whillans that your Council has put forward for an honour, he is not the gentleman who appears in the newspapers for fighting with policemen, is he?"

"Yes, ma'am, he is!" I had, reluctantly, to agree.

"Goodness, gracious, we cannot have such a man getting an honour, it would be a terrible example." And the lady secretary from the Honours Office rang off. When the list was published later that year, Joe got an MBE, but Don's name was missing.

He was later to be the subject of an Eammon Andrews *Don Whillans. This is your life* programme, and had meetings with the Duke of Edinburgh and Margaret Thatcher. I am happy to report that I was a witness at both of these truly memorable events.

They both occurred in the period when Don was a Vice-President of the BMC. The meeting with the Duke took place in May, 1978 at an informal reception in the Mansion House, London, to mark the 25th Anniversary of the climbing of Mount Everest. By that time I had met the Duke of Edinburgh on several occasions as a member of the Executive of the CCPR, since he was our President; he vaguely knew who I was, and that I was connected with the BMC. At this gathering were representatives of the Government, the Opposition, the Sports Council, the CCPR, captains of industry and so forth. The Duke slowly made his way round the vast hall, stopping for a word here, a chat there, a drink with the Minister of Sport, a word in the ear of Lord Hunt – the usual boring pleasantries that are such a feature of life in the crinkly world of the capital. Don and I placed ourselves near the drinks table, which was laden to overflowing with *Moet et Chandon*, bloody good champagne. There was a flunky in a flunky's outfit, keeping us supplied. Don was taking his draught, two glasses at a time, from the tray proffered at regular intervals. Much to his disgust, there was no beer. "Bloody gnat's piss!" he declared as he downed his dozenth glass, looking for all the world like Andy Capp with his flat cap stuck jauntily on his head, a check shirt, baggy pants and desert boots. Just then I caught sight of the Duke coming our way.

"Good evening, sir!" I sycophantically smiled.

"Ahh, it's the representative from the BMC," he responded.

"Allow me, sir, to introduce Don Whillans, one of the BMC's Vice-Presidents," I said, pointing to The Villain as I did so.

The Duke looked at Whillans and replied, "Don Whillans. Yes, I have heard of you!" with a mischievous smile and a glint in his eye.

"Ahh-doo," said Whillans, and proffered his hand, which the Duke took and shook vigorously, much to the obvious amazement of his entourage of security men and old buffers , for no one else that evening had been so bold, just a lot of bowing and scraping – but that was never The Villain's style.

In the summer of 1977 an invitation arrived on my desk at the BMC to meet the Rt. Hon. Margaret Thatcher when she was leader of the Opposition. She and her advisers were holding a series of meetings with sports bodies to ascertain what they might wish to see included in the Tory manifesto for the forthcoming election. (It did not actually happen until 1979). They had already met the Football Association, the Rugby Football Union, the Royal Yachting Association and many other national bodies, and now it was to be our turn. After consulting Alan Blackshaw, who was then an Under-Secretary in the Department of Energy and a former BMC President, it was decided that Don should accompany me on this mission to Whitehall. Alan's advice was that Margaret might be the next Prime Minister (which seemed incredible to me then) and that she would wish to meet a grass-roots mountaineer; and that nobody fitted this description better than Don. When we arrived at The Houses of Parliament on the appointed day, there was a series of votes taking place in the lobbies and our appointment was delayed. A secretary met us in the entrance and thoughtfully arranged for us to wait in a nearby pub until the great lady was free. This hostelry was instructed to charge our drinks bill to Conservative Central Office. It was the era of the 'Lib-Lab' pact and the lobbies continued all afternoon: it was to be many pints later before we were led through the stone corridors of Westminster and into the great lady's office. She was still not there and we were ushered in to sit and wait – I perched on a hard-backed chair but Don,

expansively, onto a couch. As he sank down, I realised that his flies were
open, and soon my fascinated attention drew the eyes of the attendant
lackeys – both, fortunately, male. The Villain held the floor with a tale about
a recent Himalayan epic, and was not in a mood to brook interruption.
Minutes ticked by, and any second the lady might sweep into our angst-
ridden midst, but none of us could stop the flow.

"Bloody hell, I'll have to tell him," I had decided, when one of the
secretaries suddenly leaned forward and hissed, "Mr Whillans, Mr Whillans
... you're undone ... You're undone!" with his voice rising an octave at the
end. Don stopped mid-sentence, looked down, then calmly zipped himself
up and said with a chuckle, "Tha need not have worried, yer know. Dead
birds never fall out of their nests!"

The next second, in swept Margaret and her advisers. She was not like her
media and public image, for she was younger and more attractive than I had
imagined. After the usual introductions, she was content to do more
listening than talking, politely inviting us to put forward our views about what
was needed to help our sport prosper and develop. It was obvious that she
was well-briefed and bloody clever, but that underneath she was a politician
to her well-manicured finger nails, and furthermore that her time was at a
premium and she would not spend her days making small-talk. This was, of
course, before her 'Iron Lady' image and subsequent handbagging of the
Europeans. Whillans seemed to like her, and as we walked out of the room,
he joked, "It's a pity you could not have been in the pub this afternoon,
ma'am. But thanks for the drinks!" To which Margaret replied in her best
regal manner, "I'm sorry, too, that I could not have been with you, Mr
Whillans." But somehow I thought I detected a lack of sincerity in her voice.
As we walked out of the Palace of Westminster, Don turned to me and said,
"I wonder what your old man would have said today, when that secretary
leaned over to tell me me flies were undone?"

"Exactly the same as you, yer bugger!" I joked, "I've heard that old one-
liner from everybody from the Minister of Sport (Denis Howell) to Chubby
Brown!"

The 1970s gave way to the 1980s and Don and Audrey moved to live on
the North Wales coast, where they opened a guest-house near Colwyn Bay.
Don broadened his interests during those two decades to take in many other
activities besides mountaineering, such as sub-aqua, parachuting and
breeding tropical fish. From his earliest expedition days he had shown a keen
concern with the development of equipment and, over the years, there
appeared from his fertile imagination the Whillans Box, the Whillans

Don Whillans scuba diving in the Red Sea, investigating the wreck of *The Umbria*.
Photo: J Jackson

Whammer and the Whillans Rucksack. But his most enduring contribution was the sit-harness which bore his name: the first and most important in its day of what has now become, with many new and adapted designs, an essential piece of equipment for rock-climbing – although he originally conceived the idea of a sit-harness for Himalayan mountaineering. His new interests took him on diving trips to the Red Sea; a journey through the Okavango Swamp in Botswana; a visit to the West Indies, and a parachute course, after which he joked that he fell through the skies 'like a meat safe', besides lecture tours to Australia, South Africa and the USA. He was always planning for some journey or expedition and always had a project in mind. His one enduring enthusiasm, though, was for motor-cycling, and latterly he owned several different types of bike. Perhaps this, in the end was his undoing.

The stories continued to build, and the epics to happen. For instance, when he first moved to North Wales, there was the incredible business of the

Yak. On moving to the Principality, he decided that Audrey and he would need a four-wheel-drive vehicle and purchased a Yak. That same afternoon, after arriving in Colwyn Bay and with Audrey aboard, he decided to test its capability on the rough ground of the nearby beaches. All seemed to be going well until, driving along at speed he came upon an unseen, deep pool of sea water, into which the vehicle plunged and stuck. Happily, neither he nor Audrey was hurt, but they had some difficulty in climbing out of the wallowing Yak. Once on terra firma Don ran for help, whilst Audrey stood guard, but, by the time he returned with a towing vehicle, the tide had come in and the Yak was under the water. Later that night, once the tide had retreated, it took several of the Llanberis climbing fraternity, with ropes attached to their cars, to pull it out of its sandy grave. However, despite the engine having been buried under many feet of salt water and sand for several hours, Don and a friend, Ron Dutton, completely overhauled the Yak and managed to get it running again. At the time of The Villain's death it was still driveable.

He was on Shivling in 1981, and on Broad Peak in 1983 (when Pete Thexton died so tragically of pulmonary oedema); and the following year he was on Cloggy's *Great Slab* with Bill Peascod when the Cumbrian died of a heart attack. These losses left their mark and he became ever more philosophical, more avuncular, more leisurely. A lot of his days were spent visiting old friends, and I would sometimes come home from meetings in London, Newcastle or Manchester to find him asleep in front of the fire or, if awake, spending his time in teaching my young daughter how to do a forward roll across our front room carpet – this despite his huge, Sumo-like girth.

The winter and spring of 1984/85 found him back where he had started – working as a plumber in the Manchester area, in order to eke out a living in the closed season for the guest-house. I saw quite a lot of him at the time and, just before he left for the Dolomites in the summer, he arrived in the BMC office one day in a terrible temper. He had just suffered what must have been the very last of his brushes with trouble-seekers. It transpired that whilst riding along the Mancunian Way on his way to the BMC, a car with four young men aboard had pulled in on him and knocked him into the barriers at the side of the motorway. Miraculously unhurt, and though by 1985 grossly overweight and unfit, he had picked up his motorbike, jumped back on and given chase.

"Did you catch them?" I asked, as he sat in my office, swigging a mug of tea, marks of the conflict all over his puffed-up face.

Don Whillans, the consummate motor cyclist on his Triumph near the summit of Ben Nevis.   Photo: Mrs Audrey Whillans

"Yer, I did. I caught up, passed them and then pulled the bike in front of their car. They either had to run me over or stop!"

"Bloody hell, Don, sounds like the Dukes of Hazard! What happened then?" I ventured to enquire.

"Once they'd stopped, I went up to the car, and they must have felt very secure, it being four of them to one of me. But I soon changed that. I was in such a temper, I hit the driver so hard, I flattened him. After that none of the others would get out of the car and fight. They locked all the doors and I couldn't get in at 'em – but I frightened 'em! I kicked the hell out of the bodywork with me heavy boots on! Then I rode off!"

"Jesus, Don! Nothing's changed, has it?" I gasped. He looked at me for a moment and, by now totally calm and serene, observed with a grin, "Aye, Slippery Jim, tha's reight ... nothing's changed!"

A few weeks later he went off to the Dolomites on his motor-cycle and, after visiting old haunts for a last time, set out home towards the end of July, aiming to get back in time for the 1985 British Grand Prix at Silverstone. He never made it, for the weather was atrocious and the driving conditions worse. Perhaps pushing through too hard, by the time he got to Oxford he felt ill and stopped off at a friend's. That night he died peacefully in his sleep of a heart attack. And so ended the career of the most talked-about, outstanding, all-round British mountaineer of his or any other generation. As my mother observed one night in 1964 after a disagreement in The Wise Owl in Cookridge, Leeds, when Don had been on the side of the angels, stepping in and stopping an ugly situation from developing, "Yer man Don Whillans, he's one hell of a man!" She was right, and no doubt it will be a long time before we see his like again in the climbing fraternity.

Chapter Five

Others have a story to tell

During the 1950s I was fortunate to know and climb with many outstanding personalities; some well-known, others not so familiar. Among the latter was one of my earliest schoolfriends at the Quarry Mount Primary School. His name was Peter Brown, but we gave him the nickname 'Gorilla'. Together we used to clear the snow off our pitch in Bedford Field in order to practice cricket, so keen were we on that summer game; but, once I moved to Grammar School, we drifted apart until he also became interested in climbing in the mid-50s. By that date he was mad keen on motor-cycles and worked in a garage. A short while later he raced in the Clubman's TT and on Oliver's Mount. He used to transport me of a summer's evening to Almscliff after work, and on the last section up to the Crag, by the way of a narrow lane, on a particularly acute right-hand, uphill bend, crouching down on the pillion and leaning, my foot always scraped along the ground, however high I tried to lift it.

Gorilla was older than myself, extremely strong, tall, dark and sinewy; and behind the wheel of a car, or driving a bike, he was utterly fearless; whereas on the rock-face he was timid and happy to let others lead him. I was very much in awe of his 'biking skills, for in comparison with my other climbing friends, his driving was smooth, effortless and much faster! He once let me have a go on his racing bike, a tuned Triumph 650cc, outside my parents' house in Woodhouse. As I set off for Caley Crags I missed a gear, opened the throttle too wide, and the next instant the bike shot out from under me and I hit the ground with a bone-crunching thump. Lying in the road, I watched, fascinated, as the roaring Triumph, throttle open, shot up the main road like a thing possessed until, a hundred yards later, it also suddenly fell over. Gorilla never let me near the controls of his bike again!

By 1957 he had built a couple of cars. One was an Austin Six special, the other a custom-built sports car. The former was eventually to create quite a local media stir, for it had a V8 engine under its bonnet, and all-round Allard suspension, but looked like a family saloon car. Gorilla loved to drive sedately along the A1 until a high-performance car, such as an XK Jaguar, overtook him, when he would go after it and pass the XK and its startled owner. A cat-and-mouse game would ensue over several miles, which usually ended with Gorilla putting his foot flat on the accelerator and leaving

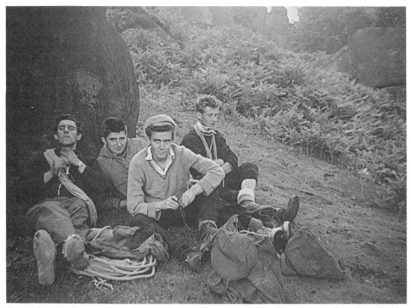

Pete 'Gorilla' Brown, Eric Beard, Dennis Gray and Mike Drysdale at Brimham Rocks, 1957.   Photo: Gray coll.

the surprised high-performance car driver in his wake as he roared off at over 100 mph. This led to letters to the newspapers, and appeals on the local radio from irate Jaguar owners whom he had passed as to, "What was the mystery vehicle, and who is the driver?" It took them quite a while to track Gorilla down and find the Austin at the garage in Woodhouse where he worked. When they did, they were not pleased, having paid thousands of pounds for their motors, whilst the Six was mainly bits and pieces.

I introduced Gorilla to Eric Beard, and at the Easter of 1957 they decided to go to North Wales together in his sports car. Gorilla had a theory that it was quicker to journey via Holme Moss over the Pennines to Chester, than the then more usual route via Huddersfield and Manchester. (This was before the M62 motorway was built.) This meant that they had to travel high over the moors, and by the time they reached the hill of Holme Moss, it was evening; darkness and snow made it difficult to see the road from the bucket seats of the sports car; nor were they sure of their route. The force of the blizzard increased and the snow fell thicker and thicker, but eventually they reached a signpost, standing as a lone sentinel in the night, obviously the answer to their route-finding problems but seated as they were, they could not read it.

"Beardie, can you get out and find the direction to Holme Moss?" Gorilla asked his passenger.

"OK, pal," declared Eric, typically full of energy; but, unthinking as he climbed out of the sports car, let his side door swing, and, 'Crack' it blew off its hinges and disappeared into the night; such was the force of the wind. After that, as the snow blew all over them, they could see neither the road nor the signpost.

"We must find the door!" decided Gorilla, and they both climbed out of the car to search for it. But without a strong light in a maelstrom of swirling, blinding spindrift, they could hardly see each other, never mind find the car door.

"We need to get a powerful light," Gorilla shouted into the wind to Beardie.

"Let's go to that farm up on the hillside and ask if they have a storm lantern." With some difficulty they climbed up a track, through the wind and driving snow to arrive to the sound of barking dogs, at a heavy door, which marked the front of the farmhouse.

They knocked loudly and insistently for a long time before they heard the sound of bolts being slid out of their sockets, to the accompaniment of much swearing and grumbling. Finally the door swung open to reveal the huge figure of a man framed in the entrance by the inside light.

"What der yer want?" he demanded in a most unfriendly tone.

"Have you a light? I need a light ....." Gorilla started to explain but got no further.

"Who the hell d'yer think I am, Florence Nightingale?" demanded the farmer, and slammed the door in their faces.

We met them two days later in the Llanberis Pass, for they had ended up that night bivouacking where they were on Holme Moss. By the time they had found the missing door, the engine refused to start and Gorilla had had to strip down the carburettor before it would go again. This had taken up most of the next day, necessitating another night's camping in that inhospitable place. It had needed all of his considerable mechanical skills to get his vehicle going again, but when we finally met up at the Grochan's field, he still maintained that his route would have been faster if he had not lost his car door. Shortly after this incident, he stopped climbing to concentrate first on motor-cycles, and later on sports car racing.

Another of my school friends was Brian 'Spider' Evans who, like me, had started climbing as a schoolboy. When I returned to Leeds from the APO in early 1956, he introduced me to Allan Austin, who at that date had literally only been climbing for a few months. We first met at Almscliff Crag and I had never before met his equal in the intensity of his approach to the sport. He was, I learned, from Thornton near Bradford, and worked for his father in the wool waste business. Powerful, dark-haired, of medium height and with a bespectacled, owl-like face, Allan loved to talk for hours about climbs, comparing route with route, move with move; which, I confess, I found boring. Even when we used to visit the Bradford Jazz club on a Monday evening to listen to the Yorkshire Jazz Band, he would be shouting out his opinion as to the merits of some climb or other above the noise of the music. At our first meeting, however, I was immediately impressed by his drive and ambition for, although he was only a novice, he had his sights set on the hardest climbs, and with Brian had just completed an early repeat of the North-West Girdle at Almscliff – which few other people of such experience would dare to attempt today, never mind in 1956. I immediately nicknamed him Tubby, for so he appeared to me. It was some time before I found out that he suffered permanently from the cold and that wearing many wool jumpers made him look stout when, in all truth, he was of a very athletic build. He also wore heavy shoes with vibram soles, in which he occasionally climbed. He told me that during his national service he had been excused boots, and so we also called him The Yorkshire Shoe Champion.

A third member of this climbing team was Doug Verity, with whom I was later to become very friendly, and whom I introduced to the Rock and Ice. Brian and Allan recruited him because they would often get stuck in those early gritstone days; and Doug, who was over six feet tall, large in build and physically strong, could stand with the palms of his hands held flat above his head onto which they could retreat or jump down! I was also glad of this ability and benefited from it on occasion when retreating off outcrop routes. (I have already recounted the incident when Doug caught Joe Brown and me upon the collapse of our human pyramid up Long John's Slab at Froggat Edge.)

Allan was almost a stereotype of the professional Yorkshireman and, apart from my paternal grandfather, he was the only person I have ever heard call money 'brass' and use the exclamation, "Eeh bah gum!" I first heard him utter these expressions on our first climbing trip together. I left my van at his father's house and we travelled to North Wales and back along with several other passengers (including Allan's future wife, Jenny) in his large Bedford, which could carry a whole climbing team of six to ten persons. On arrival back at Thornton, after a careful reckoning, he announced that I owed him 13s, 11½d. petrol money. After counting out the cash, I handed over 14

Allan Austin bouldering at Almscliff, 1959. 'Excused boots' – wearing vibram-soled shoes instead.
Photo: D Gray

shillings and, despite my protestations, he insisted on handing me back my
change – a halfpenny which, even then, would not have bought anything.

"Eeh bah gum, it's brass that counts, lad!" he insisted as he handed it
over.

This climbing group also included Brian Fuller: tall, slim, dark-haired,
and a very underrated climber. He was also extremely well-dressed, and
because of his sharp turn-out, I initially, not knowing his name, called him
Fred the Ted. Spider was actually the star of this group; but it was Austin
who had the drive and energy necessary to pioneer difficult, new routes.
From his earliest climbing days he strove towards new or difficult routes,
often getting completely out of his depth or escaping from harrowing falls
miraculously without serious injury. I was with him on several occasions
when he had narrow squeaks. One was on his first attempt at leading *The
Western Front* at Almscliff. He had previously tried this on a top rope and
failed, and on another occasion had needed a tight rope to climb the hard
moves up the crack once he had pulled over the crux overhang.

"I'll lead it!" he decided on his third attempt. I was surprised by this
decision for it had needed quite a lot of G-sharp on the rope for him to get
up it at all, and I tried to talk him out of it. He was not to be dissuaded,
however, and with me holding his rope, tied down to a boulder at the foot of
The Great Western route, he set forth. He climbed up under the roof, fingered
a small undercut, then leant out and swung his body into space, hanging by a
hold on the lip of the overhang. He pulled up, managed to get a good hand-
jam and tried to climb up and over the ceiling. But then he started to struggle
and tire.

"Oh, my God, he's going to come off!" I guessed. He was trying to reach
some higher holds, but to no avail, suddenly, he let go, and down he came,
flying through the air. He hit a prow, sticking out of the rock on which I was
standing, with his spine, and then disappeared down a gap on the other side
of the boulder, landing with a loud smack which I heard from my perch.

"Allan, Allan!" I screamed, "are you OK?" There was no answer. In a
blind panic I untied and ran round to find him sprawled over a hole in the
ground, unconscious.

"Allan, Allan, speak to me, for God's sake!" Eventually he opened his
eyes, shook his head and declared slowly, "Eeh bah gum, I'll lead it next
time!"

Miraculously, he escaped unhurt from this terrible fall, and later, in 1958,
he did manage to lead *The Western Front* which, by then was one of the
hardest outcrop climbs in the country. With such determination, it was

Brian 'Spider' Evans pioneering at Hetchell Crag near Leeds in 1962.   Photo: W Todd

Dougie Verity leading Mutiny Crack, Burbage North, 1957.   Photo: D Gray

obvious that he would end up either dead or famous, and happily it was to be the latter. In fact, during the next two decades, he was to establish himself historically as one of the most outstanding rock-climbing pioneers in the history of the sport.

However, this determination must have been hard won mentally in the early days of his climbing career; sometimes, at weekends, he would suffer from terrible nightmares. I was with him in Derbyshire when he threw a whole hut full of hardened cragsmen into a panic. It occurred when we were staying in the Rock and Heather hut (alas, no more) in Baslow, behind the Prince of Wales public house. The sleeping arrangements were in bunks and Allan was on the top tier (they were three high). I was lying on the middle, and Spider on the bottom one. Inside the hut there was total darkness, and sometime in the early hours of the morning I was woken by my bed shaking as if on board a ship in a storm. Initially, woken from a deep sleep, I was not sure where I was. Then, from above my head, came shouting: "Watch me, I'm coming off!" I immediately recognised Allan's voice. "I'm off! ... I'm off!

... I'm off!" There followed an incredible scream, and he came toppling out
of his bunk and hit the floor of the hut with a tremendous thump, where he
lay screaming and writhing for a few moments before lapsing into total
silence. By this time the hut, full of Rock and Heather members, was in total
panic, with people shouting from their bunks, "What's up?" "What the hell
is happening?" Is there a fire?" Finally, somebody managed to switch on the
lights to reveal a body on the floor, deep inside a sleeping bag. Anxious
hands turned him over, and once again I fully expected Tubby to be
suffering from serious injuries; but instead he lay there still fast asleep,
perfectly composed. He was probably dreaming his way up *The Wall of
Horrors* at Almscliff, a most significant route, of which he made the first
ascent four years later, and which already featured in his sports plan.

Doug Verity was, in character, entirely the opposite of Allan and Brian,
and acted almost as a foil to what I felt was their exaggerated approach to
climbing, being by today's standards positively 'laid-back'. Doug was
extremely sociable, an all-round sportsman who loved a pint of beer and a
good crack in the pub, and able at activities as diverse as cricket, golf (he is
still a club professional) and playing the clarinet. He was also no mean
climber in his day, but preferred to act in a back-up capacity, as a sort of
solid and immovable anchor, whose strength often saved the day when things
went wrong. His father was Hedley Verity, the legendary Yorkshire and
England spin bowler, who was built like the proverbial brick house but
perished tragically in the war. Dark and cheerful in looks, Doug's attitude to
climbing was very much like my own, and we struck up an immediate
friendship. My earliest memory of him is of our first meeting in 1956
climbing at Ilkley and then going along to a pub afterwards. We were
followed in there by a lady, a major in the Salvation Army, who came into the
bar selling *The War Cry*. On the front cover was a large photograph of a
cricketer batting at the crease, facing up to a ball that was about to hit either
his bat, or his head. With a laugh, Doug pushed a banknote into her
collecting tin, and took several copies of her newspaper.

"Thank you my son. God bless you. Remember the evils of drink!" she
reminded us.

"We will, we will!" we assured her, as she moved on to the next table. It
was only after she had gone that I realised that the cricketer on the front
cover of *The War Cry* was Doug himself.

Because of Doug's interests in music, Eric Beard's strong singing voice
and my own slight bent at playing a washboard (I played various musical
instruments badly in my youth), we formed a skiffle group together. These

were all the rage in that period. We had a Rington's tea chest bass, a clarinet and a washboard; we dressed in topees, which Doug's father had brought back from Poona whilst on a pre-war cricket tour, and long gabardine raincoats, all of which we transported to North Wales one weekend to give a performance on the Grochan's field on the Saturday evening after climbing. I recall meeting Nat Allen in Derbyshire shortly after and hearing about one of his friends, Nip Underwood, who had been to The Pass the weekend before. On arrival at the Grochan's field, where he had intended to camp, he had been amazed to find it had been taken over by a crowd of bloody idiots, dressed up in topees and playing skiffle music – and he had moved up to camp high on Snowdon to avoid the crowds, for our performance did attract an audience. Nat was gobsmacked when I confessed that it was us, and he advised us to leave the instruments at home in future, lest some irate cragsman smash them up.

As a young climber in the mid-50s, I was not used to drinking much alcohol. One Friday night in the winter of 1957, approaching the festive season, I picked Doug up from his home in Yeadon and drove out to Gargrave, where we stopped off at a pub, the landlord of which was an old cricketing friend of Doug's father. After a pint there, we drove on to Slaidburn to meet Brian Fuller, who was actively pioneering difficult new routes on West Yorkshire gritstone. We met him in a pub, where he was celebrating the forthcoming Christmas season with his workmates. The prior arrangement had been that we should pick him up there and drive up to Malham for the weekend, where we intended to prospect at Gordale Scar for new routes. Inevitably, when we arrived at the public house, drinks were pressed on us, and I am ashamed to say that we left the hostelry a little the worse for wear, to drive along the minor roads up the Dales to Malham. Our arrival and parking by the stile on the narrow road leading up to Gordale was achieved more by good luck than able management. Several times, in my inebriated state, I very nearly hit the limestone walls bordering the road. However, my friends quickly set to work putting up our tent in a nearby field, whilst I staggered up and down the road, trying to sober up before crawling into my sleeping bag for the night. Unfortunately, during this activity, the farmer's wife at the nearby house was awakened by barking dogs and looked out of her window; seeing a man lurching up and down the road outside her house, she called the police.

By the time the local constabulary arrived, we were tucked up in our sleeping bags, and I was almost comatose from the effects of alcohol. I awoke to the sound of angry voices outside the tent, and recognised Doug's voice answering what I took to be a local, who sounded intent on doing him harm. Normally, I would never trade blows with anyone, but, under the effects of the evil drink, I roused myself, burst out of the tent into the dark winter's night and, running at the figure who was giving Doug such a hard time, lashed out at him. As my fist was curling round I realised that it was a policeman, a sergeant! I somehow stopped its full force from hitting him, but I knocked his hat off instead. The next thing I knew, I was grabbed and jerked clean off the ground by the sergeant, a big, burly figure, whom I could hardly see. I realised then that he was not alone and that our encampment was surrounded by police officers.

"Where's your driving licence, laddie?" he demanded. I had only a learner licence at that time, and in fact drove thousands of miles without bothering with 'L' plates or a test for two years, and neither Doug nor Brian were experienced drivers. However, emboldened by drink and by the fact that it was difficult to see in the dark, once back on the ground I confidently grabbed my wallet out of my coat pocket – I had been sleeping fully clothed – pulled out the document, and gave it to the sergeant. Amazingly, he took only a cursory look before handing it back and then delivering his lecture.

"You come up here in the middle of the night, frightening local people who have to get up early in the morning to make a living. You should be ashamed of yourselves!" he observed.

"I'm sorry, but this is not a police state, you know. We are free to come and put up our tent in the middle of the night if we like!" I countered, much to the obvious dismay of my companions, who by now were apologising profusely.

"Oh, no, you're not. This is private land. It belongs to the people at the farm whom you woke up. They have told us to tell you that you must pack up and be gone at first light. And if you don't, we'll return and charge you with breach of the peace. You can think yourselves bloody lucky you're not living in a police state, or we'd clap you in jail," the sergeant scolded me.

Before I could argue further, Doug interrupted me, supported by Fred: "We'll be gone, officer, and we're sorry we've caused you and the farmer so much trouble!" At this the police took off, grumbling good-naturedly to each other about Leeds Teddy Boys coming up to the Dales and causing problems for them. I was very lucky in my choice of friends on that occasion, for without Doug's persuasive tongue and cricketing connections we might very well have been charged. The name Verity worked like a charm in those days, for Yorkshire had the greatest cricket team in the land.

By 1958 Doug had become a regular companion on Rock and Ice meets.

He kept us posted about Allan Austin's pioneering efforts in Yorkshire, for often, on mid-week summer evenings, he would accompany Tubby out to the local gritstone crags. At that period Allan was claiming that *The Shelf* (a route he had climbed at the Crook Rise outcrop above Skipton) compared with the hardest routes on gritstone, and so we badgered Joe Brown into travelling over there with us, specially to repeat the climb. On our arrival there it was not Joe who repeated the climb, making a second ascent, but myself, for *The Shelf*, although a bold lead (despite being only 35 feet in length), was not technically as hard as Allan had claimed; – I did manage to get up it with a little help from Joe, who climbed up and put in a protection chockstone high on the climb for me beforehand.

Joe, Doug and I then wandered along the crag towards Rylstone, looking for new route possibilities, and towards the end of the outcrop we found a buttress, which then had no routes up its steepest face; this was a part of Slingsby's Pinnacle. At its right-hand edge there was a detached flake lying against the face, and on its left-hand side, bounded by a chimney, there was an impressive arête. As soon as Joe saw these he became animated, and climbed up onto the flake for a better look at the climbing possibilities. We had walked along the edge in our boots and Brown, still wearing his, tentatively stepped down off the edge he had been standing on and onto the rock-face to his left. Then, with his left hand held high on a little edge and his right hand in a pocket, he proceeded to mantelshelf into this latter, bringing his right foot up into it, and stood up. Thus, the crux moves of a local classic were climbed at the first attempt; a slab followed, and then the finish by way of an easier groove.

Joe then turned his attention to the arête on the left, which, on its right side, had a shallow groove that commenced some way above the ground. This appeared to be of a high order of difficulty, and he changed into his PAs. But, try as he might, he could not get started direct from its base, for he could not reach any hand-holds (this way was climbed fifteen years later by local boy Ron Fawcett); he then decided to try to reach the groove by traversing out of Slingsby's Chimney on its left. At the first attempt he managed to get out of this by undercutting, using a hollow-sounding flake, which has long since disappeared; and he was then able to swing up and into the groove. From that position he found he could reach a hold with his left hand on the edge. Laybacking on this it appeared to Doug and me down below that all was well, for it was a feature of Brown's climbing that you never knew either how he did it, or whether he was OK. Suddenly, without warning, he shot off, his hand having slipped on the arête; his feet slithered under him, and down he came. For once, Doug was not on form and, though he tried, he failed to catch The Baron – butterfingers! Joe hit the base of the climb with a real thud. Fortunately, it was a good landing, being reasonably flat without any large protruding boulders, and it was obvious from his swearing that he was unhurt.

Lying winded on the ground, Joe looked thoughtful for a minute and then stood up. "Doug, you get on a rope and climb up the chimney. Dennis, you tie on another, and keep moving over to the right as I climb." This may sound complicated, but it is, in all truth, very simple. Joe tied onto two ropes, his hope being that, if he fell again, we would pull the ropes tight and he would be held in mid-air by the two strands pulled together.

"Give me some tension!" he commanded Doug, and the latter, wedged in the chimney, held the rope tight. Using this Joe reached high up the arête, grabbed a good hold, and stood up high with his right foot in the groove, which is such a prominent feature of the climb. The rest of the route, which Doug called the *'Small Brown'* because Joe could not reach the first hand-holds direct, was an anti-climax, and The Baron quickly climbed up the remainder of the groove and then up an easier wall above. Thus the other companion route, which he had climbed first, had to be called *'Hovis'*; and it was only a pity that we could not have found another climb alongside of equal merit to name *'Wholemeal'*. I sometimes think about the tricks that the pioneers got up to over the years: Norman Collie cutting his steps in Moss Ghyll on Scafell Crag; Menlove Edwards lassoing on *The Bow-shaped Slab* on Cloggy; and Ron Moseley inserting chockstones in the Left Wall of Dinas Cromlech; but the tactics we used on *'Small Brown'* were as clever as any, and proved a brilliant solution to the problem.

Each Christmas during the '50s the Rock and Ice headed for Wasdale Head and, as the decade progressed, more and more climbers from other parts of the country were attracted to our gatherings. We either stayed in a barn, in which we were able to organise games sessions, or camped; but we socialised in the nearby hotel, which was then under the stewardship of Wilson Pharaoh, once the world champion at Cumberland and Westmorland wrestling. He and his wife were generally tolerant of the Rock and Ice, although on occasion we did upset him with our antics. He was an awesome figure – all 6 foot 5 inches of him – especially when he vaulted the bar to admonish us for our wrong-doings. One such occasion was the night when Pat Walsh decided to give a display of fire-eating. This he did by taking a large gulp of paraffin into his mouth then forcing it out under pressure through his teeth, the jet thus formed being directed at a lighted match to

Sandstone Climbing Club Christmas meet, 1957. Coach to Borrowdale; then over Sty Head to Wasdale. Photo: D Stone

make a most impressive fireball. Pat gave this performance out in the hotel yard. He produced a large flame, but this was affected by the wind, and so Vin Betts and I decided to try to give a repeat performance inside the public bar for more dramatic effect.

We cleared a space and, taking a gulp of paraffin, simultaneously blew through a flame from a lighter held by Patsy. The effect was dramatic, and the sheet of fire we jointly produced must have been about six feet long, causing panic in the enclosed space, for the drinkers had to jump here, there and everywhere to avoid being scorched. Wilson, who had been down to his cellar to carry up a fresh beer barrel, re-entered the bar just as the flame sprouted, and it was immediately obvious that he was not pleased by our antics. He dropped his load with a bump, and in the next second he had leapt over the bar and was amongst us. He grabbed Vin and me, picked us up, one under each arm, and ran to the door, somehow opened it and literally threw us outside, sprawling headlong into the yard.

"You can come back in when you learn to behave yourselves. Meanwhile, you stay outside!" he commanded. We never tried fire-eating again inside the pub; but we did, unfortunately, continue our experiments after retiring to the tent which we had borrowed from Ned Gough (known to us as Count Neddy Gough).

This was a large model inside which you could stand upright, and we were camping in it just down the road from the hotel amongst a clump of gorse bushes. By this time it was raining and blowing a gale; but Vin and I were happily holding out lighted matches for each other and blowing our fireballs into the night through the open doorway of the tent, when Betts accidentally set fire to the canvas. Try as we might, we could not stop the flames spreading and within seconds the whole of the tent fabric was ablaze, and we had to abandon our refuge in a hurry. Naturally, it burnt down, and we damaged most of our own gear as well. Count Neddy Gough was not as annoyed as Mr Pharaoh, however, and was heard to observe laconically that fire-eating seemed to be a dangerous profession, as he watched his tent burn into ashes. The rest of the crew made room for us in their tents. Thus ended my attempts to become a fire-eater.

Twice at these festive occasions – in 1957 and 1959 – we were called out on rescues during Christmas Eve, late at night after much celebrating. In that era equipment such as stretchers was held at places like the Wasdale Head Hotel, but the actual physical task of the rescue would be performed by any group of climbers who happened to be around at the time when the call came for assistance. As can be imagined, this did not result in a well-organised team such as you will find today in Llanberis, Glencoe or Langdale. On one of my earliest trips to the Lake District in 1949 I had taken part in such an exercise when a young girl had fallen on Gimmer and been killed, and I quickly learnt that they were not occasions for mock heroics, nor were they to be taken lightly. You only turned out if you were sure there was a real need. I also remember being at Wasdale Head one Saturday evening in the 1950s, when a climber known to us came into the barn as we were cooking our supper, and asked us to go out and help him look for his two mates.

"When did they set out to go climbing?" demanded Alfie Beanland, my older companion.

"At lunch-time," responded the worried climber.

"Bloody hell, man, they've not had time to get lost yet!" advised Alfie. "If they're not back by morning, then we'll go out and look for them." And sure enough, they came staggering into the barn in the early hours of Sunday morning, none the worse for the experience of being benighted on Pillar Rock.

The two Christmas rescues at Wasdale Head were different however. The first was an incident of high drama and farce; the other ended in a terrible tragedy.

On Christmas Eve, 1957 we were in the public bar of the hotel after enjoying a good day's rock-climbing in unseasonably warm and dry weather, and a loud sing-song was under way, when a young male climber came staggering into our midst in an obvious state of distress. "My girlfriend is stuck up on Westmorland Crags," he announced, which we took to be a Christmas joke, until he started sobbing and bawling like a child. Mrs Pharaoh ushered him through into her kitchen, and Ron Cummaford and I were invited in there to try to decide how to help. The lad told us his story. It transpired that he and his companion had been climbing a chimney on Westmorland Crags, which lie high above the Napes, just below the summit of Great Gable. The chimney had narrowed at one point to a crack and, in trying to follow her leader, the young woman had become jammed by her thigh, stuck in the fissure. Even as we spoke, she was alone up there, suffering agonies as she hung off her leg, waiting to be rescued. After a brandy, a cup of tea and a sandwich, the young climber assured us that he was fit enough to go back up, and Ron and I decided to assemble a group of Rock and Ice members to carry out the rescue, accompanied by the Doctor. The latter was an old medical chap who used to be in Wasdale every Christmas, and we hoped that somehow between us we could either lift or pull the poor girl out of the crack. As we left the bar in order to put on our climbing gear and collect the rescue equipment, a stretcher and other necessary items, Mrs Pharaoh had a brain-wave and handed over to us a large pat of butter with which to grease the lady's thigh as we tried to extricate her from her predicament.

It is surprising how quickly drunken climbers sober up once they start walking uphill, and what started out as a rabble, falling all over the hillside in the dark, clinging onto the stretcher and sharing turns at carrying the heavy medical rucksack as we climbed out of the Wasdale Valley, had become, by the time we reached The Napes area, a procession of sober judges, grimly determined to get the task over as quickly as possible in order to get back to the bar before it closed – despite it being a beautiful night with a nearly full moon and a myriad stars in the sky. The Doctor, however, was lagging a long way behind us as we climbed up and up above the valley, and we had to keep stopping and waiting for him, for he seemed the drunkest of the party, delaying our climb up to Westmorland Crags and our location of the poor, stuck girl. In every such situation there has to be someone who takes the lead, and on this occasion it was Ron. On reaching Westmorland Crags, despite the darkness, we could see the girl clearly from below, stuck in a crack about forty feet from the ground, hanging safeguarded by a rope above her, which had been tied off and belayed by her boyfriend before he had descended. Against all expectations she was in high spirits and shouted down to us, "What took you so long?" but it was evident from the tone of her voice that she was relieved at our arrival. Ron and I climbed up in the dark and, as soon as we got below the lady, we realised that she had rather large thighs and that the left one was stuck in the crack. Ron stood on the ledge below her, pushing upwards, while I climbed above her and pulled on the rope – but to no avail, for she really was stuck.

"Where is the butter? Who's got the butter?" demanded Ron, shouting down to the team below.

"I've got it," came the voice of Eric Beard.

"Has anyone got a sharp penknife? We need to cut her trousers and grease her thigh with butter!" decided Ron.

"I say, you can't do that," the anxious voice of her boyfriend came floating up to us.

"This is no time for prudery, is it, Doctor?" Ron countered.

"No, my boy!" shouted the man of medicine.

And so, after pulling up a rucksack with butter and a knife stowed inside, Ron started cutting and rubbing. To cut a long story short, using this method and with several of us pulling on the rope and pushing her backside at the same time, she eventually came out of the crack like a cork out of a bottle, to be lowered, minus half her trousers, into the waiting arms of her beloved, who greeted her safe return with a relieved embrace. We descended and regrouped, and after some massage from the Doc, a medicinal brandy and a short rest, the girl was able to hobble down the screes of Hell's Gate, hanging onto her boyfriend's arm without any help from us. So we of the disgruntled, makeshift rescue team had to stagger back through the night, carting the unused Thomas stretcher and heavy rucksack back to their base at the Wasdale Head Hotel, where we arrived just in time for last orders at 2am.

The rescue on Christmas Eve, 1959 started in almost identical circumstances, except for the foul weather outside, commencing when a young climber staggered into the bar, shouting that he needed a rescue party. Once again we entered Mrs Pharaoh's kitchen, and on this occasion learned that, returning to their tent high in Mosedale after visiting the bar, the lad and his girlfriend had fallen down a bank and landed in the beck, which was in spate. He had managed to extricate himself, and crawl out onto the bank, but his companion had sunk into a pool, and he had not been able to get her out, for she was unconscious. It was obvious from these details that

Ginger Cain: Leeds University student, climber, hitch-hiker and artist, in action in the early 50s.   Photo: P. Greenwood

Ronnie Cummaford, The Rock and Ice's keenest wit.   Photo: D Gray

speed was of the essence, and that there was no time for making elaborate plans. It was literally a race against time, for if the girl had not drowned she would soon die of exposure, lying in a pool of icy water. Despite the tragic circumstances, the scene that followed was hilarious: a dozen of us ran out into the dark, stormy night and, unthinking and unseeing, jumped over the wall behind the hotel, intent on crossing the stream to start running up Mosedale. First over the wall was Whillans, who leapt so high and so far out that he landed up to his waist in water, and we did not see him again until the rescue was over, for he was swept downstream. The rest of us, after witnessing his example, walked upstream to wade at a wider and shallower point, and were well on our way up the valley by the time Don had extricated himself. Besides Rock and Ice members, others present that night were the artist Ginger Cain, some members of the Sandstone and Cave and Crag Clubs, and the Doctor, who once again joined the rescue team. As on the Gable exercise, it was surprising how quickly everyone sobered up as we staggered up the rough, boulder-strewn path into Mosedale. With the help of the half-drowned young climber, we located the pool in which the girl's body was lying in about fifteen minutes. But the stream had become a river, and reaching her proved to be a dangerous problem. We could see that she was under the water, trapped by a rock-shelf and wedged there. On this occasion our appointed leader was Vin Betts from Sheffield who, despite being at times one of the most outrageous members of the Rock and Ice, was very knowledgeable in first-aid and a strong swimmer (as we knew from similar situations at Castle Rock). We had brought a Tilley lamp with us to light our way, and I must admit that, looking into the foaming stream that night by its light, with the wind screeching around us and rain pouring from the heavens, my heart sank and I was frightened. Vin tried to dive in to reach the trapped girl, but the force of the water swept him away, and he was fielded by a team of catchers whom we had stationed downstream. Then Ginger Cain (a friend from my earliest climbing days when he was a student at Leeds) came up with a brain-wave: "Let's all join up shoulder to shoulder and support each other, and wade out to reach her." And this we did, with Ginger going first, Vin second, me third, and so on. When we got out into the pool, the water was up to my waist and so cold that I could hardly breathe. But for the support of the rest of the crocodile, which eventually stretched across both sides of the stream, we would have been swept away. But Ginger managed to dive in, grab hold of the girl and free her.

Once we had her out of the beck and onto the bank, Vin and the Doctor took it in turns to give her mouth-to-mouth resuscitation, and we wrapped her in blankets which Eric Beard, who by this time had run down to the hotel and back, had carried up. We were convinced that she was still alive as we carried her down, and Vin assured us that she had started to breathe again and had shown some signs of life. But once in Mrs Pharaoh's kitchen, while we waited for the ambulance to arrive, despite non-stop efforts with mouth-to-mouth, massage and everything else the Doc and Vin could do to try to save her life, the poor girl died. It was a dreadful thing to happen at any time, but at midnight on Christmas Eve it was a shattering experience, and the girl's partner was beside himself with grief and remorse. But when I think about it now, despite the tragedy, I wish to record Ginger's bravery and initiative in recovering the body, for he, too, could so easily have become a victim.

Wasdale Head remained the tradition for us at Christmas for another couple of years after this, and the numbers attending grew and grew, but somehow it was never the same again for me after the drowning accident. Our gatherings were finally disrupted by the dispersal of the Rock and Ice around the country and abroad, when other venues took over. But at our meets two of the memorable happenings, for me, were the ascent in winter

Dez Hadlum climbing *The Corner*, Curbar Edge, 1959, watched by Doug Scott, then a
schoolboy.   Photo: D Gray

conditions of Scafell's Moss Ghyll one Boxing Day, and my affair with 'the
Blue Baby'.

The first was memorable being one of my earliest climbs with two
companions with whom I later climbed a lot – Dez Hadlum and Doug Scott.
I was living by then in Derby and working for a firm of fine art printers,
where I made the acquaintance of these two young climbers from
Nottingham. Surprisingly, in view of their subsequent climbing achievements, Dez was the stronger climber of the pair; for instance, in 1963 he and
Joe Brown repeated the Bonatti Pillar of the Dru (including the ascent of the
couloir) in a single day. Our ascent of Moss Ghyll turned out to be a joint
effort, with Dez leading us up the lower sections of the climb to the Tennis
Court ledges, and myself leading the famous Collie's Step, in which I cut
nicks in the ice for hands and feet with the spike of a piton hammer; then
Doug took over and swam up the exit cracks, gleefully shouting down, "It's
just like the Eigerwand up here!" After finishing the climb, however, getting
down from the summit of Scafell proved more dangerous than the ascent,
and we almost ended up in Eskdale, descending in darkness and snowy
conditions.

The affair of 'the Blue Baby' was different, and pure joy – for she was a

The Sandstone CC at Wasdale Head Barn, 1958. Clockwise from top left: Dave Fagan, Paul
Smoker, Phil Gordon, John Smoker, Roger Stapleton.   Photo: I Stone

beautiful and intelligent young lady with blonde hair, blue eyes and a petite
figure. I had never met anyone quite like her, and she occupied my fantasies
from the moment we were introduced. She was residing at the Wasdale
Head Hotel where, along with our friends from the Sandstone Club,
particularly Paul Smoker who was a consummate pianist, we had decided to
put on a pantomime on Christmas Day. During the rehearsals romance
blossomed between this young lady (who we all knew as the Blue Baby)
because she was always dressed in blue and myself. However, there was a
major snag in this affair of the heart, for the lady already had a strapping
young beau, whose physique would have made two of me, and whom we
immediately nicknamed The Lion Tamer, because he was dressed in
leather, including boots which almost came up to his knee-caps. On
Christmas Eve, after a last rehearsal, I managed to arrange a secret
assignation with the Blue Baby, and we enjoyed a romantic stroll on the
shores of Wastwater by the light of a sly moon. In all truth, and by today's
standards, it was an innocent affair; but unfortunately we were missed, and
later that night, the worse for drink, The Lion Tamer came looking for me,
and burst into the barn as we were playing rugby.

"You!" he shouted, pointing at me. "I want to fight you!"

"Me!" I gasped. "I'm no fighter. Can't we talk about it?" I tried to reason with him.

"You White Rose men are all the same – all talk and no action," he shouted (I guessed from this that he was a Lancastrian), and began advancing on me, obviously intent on giving me a good duffing. At this juncture, Trevor Jones from Birmingham's Cave and Crag Club, who was later to gain fame as an outstanding President of the Climber's Club, and who had until that moment been prostrate on a pile of straw in a corner of the barn, staggered to his feet and, putting up his hands in classical pugilist style, said, "I'll fight you to defend the honour of the Khaki Rose of Warwickshire!"

Trevor has a wonderful personality, and is one of the century's most amusing climbers, but on this occasion his sense of humour turned out to be misplaced. The Lion Tamer, roaring like a whipped beast, leapt through the air at him and carried him down with the sheer force of his charge; and as he did so I was certain I could hear a loud 'snap'. Our rugby game that evening had been a contest between the Rock and Ice and the Sandstone Club and for some reason everyone decided, as Trevor went down, that this was a signal to join in a two-team scrum, forgetting about the ball. I stood by, aghast, as Phil Gordon, Whillans, Ron Cummaford, the Smokers and many more piled on top of Trevor and his assailant. I could hear Jones screaming, but it took the rest of us a long time to stop the fighting, and last to be restrained was The Lion Tamer, whose face by this time looked like a squashed tomato, so bloody had it become – but it still took about half a dozen pairs of strong arms to hold him.

"Bloody hell!" Once the mass of bodies had been cleared, it was obvious that Trevor was badly hurt. He had passed out and his leg was crumpled under him. Once again, the Doctor was summoned out of the bar, and he quickly confirmed the obvious. In the early hours of the morning we had to take Jones to Whitehaven Hospital. The next night, after his return from casualty, and during our pantomime performance, he received the loudest cheer of the evening as he made a guest appearance, staggering across in front of the audience displaying his badly fractured leg in a huge plaster cast. I decided after this to abandon my hope of romance with the Baby Blue, and politely ignored her for the rest of the evening. Instead I spent some time befriending and buying a few drinks for The Lion Tamer to make my changed aspirations clear; he who is scared easily lives longer.

It is surprising how the writing of a climber's name will sometimes bring to mind a long-forgotten incident; and so, with the recording of Trevor Jones' name, an event comes vividly to my mind. I saw quite a lot of him in the 1950s in North Wales, and we were both members of a party of British climbers who visited the Dolomites in 1960. He is one of the outstanding personalities of the climbing scene and although he actually has a most impressive climbing record, somehow looks most unlikely to be a hard climber, being short and dumpy in physique but always surrounding his activities in good humour and laughter. One of Trevor's most enduring foibles is absent-mindedness, and this led to 'the affair of the missing PAs', which commenced when I picked him up and gave him a lift one Sunday night back down the Llanberis Pass after a day's climbing. I dropped him at his own vehicle but, once he had driven away, I realised that he had left his rock boots behind – a very important omission in that period, for no-one could afford more than one pair. On the following Friday night, when he arrived to join us at the Grochan's field after driving from Birmingham, he was bemoaning the fact that he had lost his PAs and that, if he could not get another pair, his climbing activities would be circumscribed. Magic Boots, as they were then colloquially known, were hard to come by: climbing shops were few and far between in those days.

"I have a spare pair in my van you can try on if you like?" I assured him, thinking that he would immediately recognise the boots as his own. But no, I was confounded by his grateful comment to me after trying them on, "They fit me as well as my own pair did!"

I insisted he return them on the Saturday evening, which he dutifully did, and on the Sunday morning lent them to him again, on the understanding that he brought them back once more that evening. This saga carried on throughout another weekend, but on the following Saturday, after Trevor had been climbing and was sitting in my van with a brew in his hands, for some reason he turned the boots over and looked under the tongue of one of them. There, marked in faint pen, was the legend 'C. T. Jones'.

"You bastard, you Yorkshire swine, these are my own boots!" he gasped.

"Yeh, I know," I replied. Fortunately, Trevor has always been able to take a joke against himself, and he laughed out loud with the rest of the Rock and Ice who were sitting in my vehicle.

In the summer of 1959 I climbed with several members of the Sandstone Club in Wales, and was subsequently invited in the autumn to visit them at their hut at The High Rocks near Tunbridge Wells, to climb on the outcrops of south-east England. The occasion in question was their Annual Dinner, and several Rock and Ice members, including Vin Betts and Ron Cummaford, made the journey south with me, driving down the A1 through

Phil Gordon just before he came off with the
flake, *Left Wall*, Cenotaph Corner, 1959.
Photo: D Gray

Dennis Gray on *Advertisement Wall*, 1959.
Photo: A Mayes

London on the Friday night. Our hosts were awaiting our arrival at the entrance to the rocks around the midnight hour. Phil Gordon and Martin Boysen introduced us to Julie and Terry Tullis, Billy Maxwell, Paul and John Smoker, John Turner, Mike Davies and a host of other London climbers, including Ernie (who was actually a girl). I had climbed with Phil and Martin quite a lot that summer in North Wales, Derbyshire and Yorkshire. One of our climbs had been an epic – the third ascent of the Left Wall on Dinas Cromlech. It had taken a whole day of siege tactics before I finally managed to lead the last section, not before Phil had taken a massive fall lower down, when a flake which had broken off under his weight had nearly hit Martin. Had it done so, Britain would probably have been deprived of the man who became one of the leading climbers of the '60s, for it was a huge piece of the crag that broke away. Moreover we would have lost our pancake maker, for Martin's great culinary forte in that period was crêpes. The hut turned out to be an amazing place. It was built into a crevice in the rocks and, in its woodland setting, looked like Hansel and Gretel's cottage. It was perhaps typical of many other such climbers' howff of that period – dank and dark inside, but providing shelter and a meeting place for

Sandstone CC hut, High Rocks, in the early 50s.   Photo: D Stone

contact with other like-minded souls. Climbing has now lost that sense of
wonder and romanticism, which disappeared with the advent of ease of
transportation, and the development of the climbing media and guidebooks,
plus the publication of the many 'how to do it' manuals. These have slowly
leached the last vestige of mystery out of our once, but now no more, secret
society.

On the Saturday we climbed at Harrison's Rocks, near Groombridge (a
place I was later to know well, for it is managed by a joint BMC/Sports
Council committee of which I was a member for many years). However, on
this first visit we had great difficulty in following our hosts up their different
party pieces. I climbed with Martin Boysen and Phil Gordon, and I can still
remember struggling up *Niblick*, *Edward's Effort* and the *Unclimbed Wall* on
tight ropes. But the one climb whose every move I still recall vividly is *Slim
Finger Crack*. I soloed this route after making the initial layback moves, then
being totally committed and unable to retreat, made the long reaches above
these to reach edges on which to make some further difficult laybacks. The
loose sand lying around on the rock surface undermined my confidence, and
I very nearly fell off whilst pulling over the top of this route; but, as I did so,
the story of Whillans' ascent in similar circumstances came to mind.
Standing at the bottom of the climb before he had set forth, he had declared

Martin Boysen on *Inspiration*, Bowles Rocks.   Billy   Maxwell   on   *Slim-finger*   *Crack*,
Photo: T Tullis   Harrison's Rocks, in the mid-50s.
Photo: D Stone.

aloud to his shocked hosts: "This looks like a scruffy little route?" but, after struggling up the climb and returning safely to terra firma, he acknowledged, "It is a HARD scruffy little route!"

However, these sentiments do not reflect my own on the outcrop, and it remains for me, a favourite place to climb, placed as it is amidst woodland, and with extensive views away over the undulating farmlands of the Sussex countryside, dotted with oast and manor houses. We quickly found out, during these initial climbs, that the sandstone outcrops of the south-east, although similar in scale to the gritstone crags of the Pennines, are of much softer rock, and so the friction is not as good; but because of the top-rope techniques usually employed before leading a climb, they boasted some of the hardest routes in the country.

At the dinner held in the High Rocks Hotel on the Saturday evening, we also discovered that, despite our own parochial ideas about the superiority of northerners over southerners (particularly Londoners), the Sandstone members had outstanding performers at everything from speech-making, singing, playing musical instruments, rough game sessions and drinking.

128   TIGHT ROPE

Paul Smoker impressed us with his witty, after-dinner climbing songs and
piano playing and he was, I believe, the equal of Tom Patey in that field.
Their games were as dangerous as any I have ever seen, and Billy Maxwell, a
small, dark-haired, athletic martial arts specialist, beat the band at diving
over chairs; I seem to remember that his record was thirteen wooden chairs.
The competition commenced with everyone diving over one, then two, then
three, to land on a carpet, but after that number we rapidly dropped out, and
by the time it got to about ten chairs in line, only Billy was left in the contest.
To my thinking, this was an incredibly dangerous pastime, for if you
misjudged your leap and hit the top of the chair backs with your chest, you
would have been lucky not to fracture your ribs. Vin Betts upheld the Rock
and Ice's honour by winning the limbo dancing, and we also won the wall
squatting competition, but we were totally outclassed in the drinking stakes,
and I have to confess that it was a very drunken team of northerners who
staggered back up to the Sandstone hut after downing many Poachers and
Tanglefoots.

On the Sunday, after a late start, we climbed at High Rocks, and I
remember Phil Gordon (a relation of Geoffrey Winthrop Young and a
fourth-generation climber), who is best described as powerful, leading me
up a route called *Advertisement Wall*, which was bloody hard; and then
everyone laid siege to a climb called *The Lobster* which had not yet been led.
Vin Betts had a go and achieved a surprising height for a non-sandstone
expert, for he managed to climb the crack which is a major feature of the
route, and reached the finger pocket in the wall above that – he was pulling
on this and going for the top when his feet shot off the rock, and down he
came, to hit the ground with a terrible thump, from what must have been a
height of 20 feet. Unhurt but winded, he lay spread-eagled on the ground,
gasping for breath (he suffered from asthma), slated his second man, John
Smoker, in no uncertain terms,

"Yer were supposed to catch me, yer know! Yer a bloody Cockney drink of
water!" This latter term of abuse Vin had learned from the master himself,
Don Whillans, with whom he climbed on occasion, including the first ascent
of Cloggy's *Slanting Slab.*

Many of the Sandstone Climbing Club remain friends until this day, and I
am now an honorary member of their group. The loss of Julie Tullis on K2
in 1986 was a terrible blow to us all, for she was one of the club's keenest
supporters and most outstanding characters. But one person we seem to
have lost contact with is Paul Smoker; he is, I believe, now Professor of
Peace Studies at one of the American universities. He was very active in

Paul Smoker imitating his idea of a yeti by immersing himself inside a WD jumping jacket (a de rigeur garment for climbers in the early 50s). At the Cromlech Boulders.
Photo: D Stone

Julie and Terry Tullis in the entrance to the High Rocks Inn, the scene in bygone years of much local climbing folklore. Photo: T Tullis

CND in the days when I first knew him; he went on the Aldermaston marches, and even persuaded various climbing friends to go along to such events – they returned with stories of having enjoyed a bloody good time. My keenest memory of him is of Stanage Edge in the winter of 1959, when he was seconding me after I had led *The Dangler*. He was a fine climber and, moving quickly and confidently up to the roof, which is the main feature of the climb, set 25 feet above the ground, he swung out on the lip of this crux overhang to hang full length from his hands, swinging around wildly, to the delight of a large mixed audience. Unfortunately, his gyrations broke his trouser belt, and his pants and shorts fell down far enough to reveal a naked bottom and thighs to the cheering group below. He somehow managed to climb the rest of the route with his pants around his legs and, totally unabashed, on getting to the top, but after pulling up his trousers, he shouted down to those below, "And now, for my next trick, I will swallow dive into your midst!" I was gobsmacked when he ran to the edge, looking as if he really intended to leap 40 feet onto a terrible boulder landing, but he grabbed a handhold and stopped himself at the very last moment. "Fooled yer, didn't I?" he remonstrated with his friends below, as they ran hither and thither to avoid being hit by a falling Smoker.

News reached us via Peter Biven and Trevor Peck about their explorations in Cornwall. Sea-cliff climbing was then in its infancy, and the prevailing wisdom amongst our own circle of friends was that a trip to the south-west was an eccentric adventure to an unheard-of climbing region. However, on meeting Peter and Trevor when climbing at Froggat Edge in May, 1956, The Ram and I were tempted into checking the area out. On the way down to West Penwith we blew the front tyre of the Royal Enfield Bullet on Bodmin Moor and had to bivouac in that inhospitable spot. Travelling during that decade always had a spice of adventure, and punctured tyres were a constant source of danger, for they had a different construction and usually went down abruptly. Johnny Sutherland of the Rock and Ice once had a similar experience and solved it by stuffing his damaged tyre tube with grass, on which he rode many miles before reaching a garage. There was a myth abroad in that period that the sun always shines on the Lands End area and on St Ives in particular; but for us, on that first visit, it rained most of the time; and when it was not actually raining, there were sea frets cosseting the cliffs. We climbed at Chair Ladder, Bosigran and Sennen, and the best feature of those cliffs then was that there were no other climbers around; and it was unbelievably cheap to live in Cornwall. We camped for free and ate our meals in Rosemergy Farm. Breakfasts cost 2/6d – 15p in today's money. The highlight of our trip was our meeting with A.W. Andrews, who with E.C. Pyatt had edited the first guidebook to the district, published in 1950. This was an eclectic work, putting as much emphasis on the fauna and flora of the region as on climbing, and was typical of its authors. Andrews had been an early pioneer of climbing in Snowdonia but, living as he did in Zennor, was historically the father of sea-cliff exploration. When we met him he was almost 90 years of age and frail, but he plied us for stories of our climbs and friends. "How many pitons did Brown and Whillans use on the Blatiere?" he demanded. Andrews had not only held the record for the mile in his twenties, but had also reached the men's tennis semi-final at Wimbledon. As well as being an athlete, he was also a writer and poet. One is forced to admit that 'they don't make 'em like that any more'.

Our initial casing of the Cornwall area finally convinced the Rock and Ice to travel south, and on subsequent trips to this area we met up with Trevor Peck and Peter Biven. In retrospect they were a surprising partnership: Trevor, a self-made hosiery millionaire, had discovered climbing late in life through a chance meeting had met his young partner, who had hitched a lift in his Rolls Royce out to the crags in Derbyshire. They had formed a partnership of great enterprise and initiative, based on the drive of youth allied to sage experience of life. Peck was small and wiry, Peter tall and gangling, and they were responsible for over 300 new routes throughout Britain during the period of their collaboration. Trevor was an equipment innovator; he was one of the first persons anywhere to develop stainless steel pitons to combat the ravages of salt water, and later produced some of the first wired nuts. His death from cancer in March, 1969 seemed to mark the end of an era in Cornish climbing, which was emphasised still further a few years later when Peter Biven was killed in a freak accident at the Avon Gorge. I will always remember them rolling along the lanes of West Penwith in Peck's built-especially-for-climbing motor caravan, heading for the Great Zawn, Bosigran or Chair Ladder. Trevor, a man of impeccable taste, had his own brand of tea, his own rolled cigarettes (although he himself hardly smoked at all), and carried enough pure water aboard his mobile to last a full alpine holiday. They were a remarkable duo in an outstanding period of sea-cliff exploration.

During my national service I began running, and this had remained a great interest of mine. Through it I met Eric Beard and subsequently introduced him to the hills. Barrel-chested, long-legged, with equally long but thin arms like piston rods, set on a short body of medium height, he went on to become the greatest fell runner of his generation. He was unlike most other athletes in my experience for, although no less dedicated, he was willing to keep all hours God sends. He had a strong voice and really enjoyed a good sing-song in the pub or taking part in theatricals. Towards the end of his short life he even organised his own legendary cabaret evenings – 'Beardie's Sing-Song' – twice a week during the ski season in the Cairngorms. His story is perhaps already well-known, for it was that of another young, working class lad, who left school at 14 years of age to drift through a succession of jobs and a series of leisure pursuits until he found that he was good at fell running, at which he was, without doubt, the most outstanding of his era. At the time I met him in the winter of 1955 he was a key member of the Leeds Athletic Club, and was hoping to build up a team of road runners to compete in the many such races then appearing in the athletic calendar. Over the next fifteen years I was to share many amusing and happy times running and climbing with Beardie. But what I wish to recall here are two stories, in a context of athletic events.

The first time I ever went anywhere with him was when I agreed to meet him in a transport café at Ingleton on the Saturday night before the Three

Peaks Race in the Yorkshire Dales in the winter of 1956. During the afternoon he had competed in a ten-mile road race (in which he came fifth) at Lancaster. He had travelled there in the morning by train from Leeds, a long, circuitous journey, and by the time the race had finished, it being the winter months, there were no buses across to Ingleton. But he had assured me that he would easily be able to hitch-hike the twenty miles to rendezvous with me, and that there was no need to travel over to Lancaster specially to pick him up. I had spent the Saturday climbing at Ilkley, and journeyed up in the early evening to the appointed meeting place to await Eric's arrival. Six o'clock, seven, eight, nine came and went, and I sat on in the cavernous depths of the transport café, listening to the juke box and drinking brew after brew. Outside it was cold; I hung around until I could stand it no more, and at midnight I drove off in my van to a lay-by in Chapel le Dale, where I crept into my sleeping bag inside my vehicle. I got up the next morning early, and decided that I had better check out the café in Ingleton one last time before driving up to the start of the Three Peaks Race. To my astonishment when I arrived, there sat inside, with a mug of tea at his elbow, sat Beardie.

"I couldn't get a lift so I had to walk here from Lancaster," he cheerfully informed me as I entered the café.

"I arrived at 2am and they told me you'd driven off at midnight."

"Bloody hell, Beardie, have you had any sleep?" I gasped.

"Not really, I've been sat in here all night 'cos I haven't got a sleeping bag!"

"Do you still want to run in the Three Peaks Race?" I queried,

"Yeah, course I do!" and so I drove him up to the Hill Inn in time for the start.

What followed was an amazing performance. I had not really seen him in action before that day and I realised that he only came into his own over long and ultra-long distances. Once the race was under way, he was first up Ingleborough and still in the lead up Pen y Ghent, but on the long flog over to Whernside from that peak, struggling through the bogs and coarse grass, he began to tire, and finally came home to the Hill Inn in fifth position. To say that I was impressed by this effort is an understatement, for he had already run in a ten-mile race the day before, walked over twenty miles through the night from Lancaster to Ingleton, gone without sleep and then beaten hundreds of other athletes over a 21-mile course which covers some of the roughest ground in the Pennines. I have often thought that if ever there were to be an Eric Beard memorial event, in order to do him justice it would have to include these three challenges, in the same way as he

Eric Beard running the Welsh 3000ers in May 1962. Fourteen peaks in 5 hrs 26 mins.
Photo: D Beard

accomplished them.

Beardie had more energy than anyone else I have ever met, and he had a theory that if you slowly cut down on sleep, you could almost get to the point of living a 24-hour day. He used to cheat, however, and could fall asleep in the most unlikely of places, cat-napping for a short while before bouncing back with vigour once more. One Christmas in Wasdale Head, for a joke, the lads spiked his drinks, and after that it was hell, for later that night, after everyone had retired, he lay in the barn, blind drunk, singing at the top of his voice until dawn. His energy was prodigious when doing what he liked most – namely, running and singing.

My first race with him as a member of the Leeds team was the Windermere to Kendal road race along with another club member, Freddie Barnfield. I was still only a junior (they were both seniors), but as they could not find a third member to make up the necessary numbers, I was pressed into service. We journeyed up to Kendal from Leeds in the depths of winter on Beardie's 650cc Thunderbird motor-cycle combination, and I soon realised that he was quite the worst driver I had ever been with. He seemed to have great difficulty in concentrating and several times I had to lean forward from the pillion and grab the handlebars to help with the steering as he alternately sang or talked non-stop, whilst the bike drifted all over the road. The Windermere to Kendal race was my first ever road race, and it is a tough course on which to start one's career, for it begins with an excruciating climb up a steep hill and finishes over eight miles later down a long incline. By the time I reached Kendal Town Hall I was knackered and was only kept going by Eric, who came out to run in to the tape with me, after he had already finished in the first dozen. Freddie had done well, having arrived not far behind Beardie; and thus, despite my being well down the field, we won a prize for the second team home.

It was real 'Tough of the Track' stuff in those days, and we literally had to dress at the finish, in the depths of winter, without the benefit of a hot shower or a cup of tea. Beardie had parked his Thunderbird in Kendal and we had journeyed to Windermere for the start of the race on the bus, and so after dressing we climbed aboard the combination and set forth to find the nearest chippie. After a bag of chips and a brew we joined the A65 as night set in, to drive home to Leeds, with Freddie in the sidecar, me on the pillion and Eric at the controls. Inevitably, just as we were tiring from our earlier experiences in travelling up to the race and taking part, our real ordeal was about to begin; for within a few miles of commencing our return journey, by which time darkness was complete, we ran into thick, freezing fog. Those who have never been on a motorbike in winter without proper clothing have never really felt cold. Beardie had bought the combination only a few days before, and both he and I were wearing the clothes you might then have worn on a mountain: long socks, gloves, a balaclava, tweed jacket and flannel pants; how I envied Freddie in the sidecar, snug and warm by comparison. However, all did go well with our journey, despite the icy roads and fog, until we came to the section of road leading across Clapham Common.

This is an open section of carriageway without walls, bordered by grass and moorland, and normally, on a Thunderbird, you would roar across this at the ton or thereabouts. However, despite the fact that the fog was lifting somewhat and that we could see the road ahead more clearly, we were going slower and slower and slower.

"What's wrong with the bike?" I shouted out into the freezing night, but for once got no reply. We were almost down to walking speed and by then going all over the road when I realised what the problem was – and it was fortunate that there were no other vehicles about. Eric, sitting at the controls, was fast asleep! Just at that moment we ran off the road and the combination slowly descended into a ditch. At this Beardie woke up with a jolt.

"Where am I?" he gasped.

"In a ditch near Ingleton, you comedian!" I grumbled as I climbed down off the pillion, which was up in the air like a ducking stool, for the Thunderbird had nose-dived into the stream. It took a great effort by the three of us to push the motorbike and sidecar out of this position back up onto the road, and the rest of the journey was then complicated by the fact that the front wheel of the Thunderbird was buckled. We finally arrived home in the early hours of Sunday morning, and at the first opportunity on Monday Eric sold the combination, having decided, "I'm not cut out to drive around, sitting behind the controls of high-powered machines. I prefer to go everywhere on my own two legs." These words were, to prove tragically prophetic, for almost to the anniversary of that weekend, fourteen years later, by which date he had become the holder of nearly every major fell-running record, Beardie was killed whilst a passenger in an MGB sports car being driven at speed down the M6. He had spent the weekend in the Lake District and was on his way back to Liverpool, where he was to make an attempt later that week on the world 24-hour distance running record at the Walton track.

It is a good job that none of us knows what the fates have in store for us,

Early attempts on chalk. Ned Cordery
hammering in a home-made piton at Oxted in
1954.   Photo: A Mayes

Mervyn at Ogwen Falls tea-hut in the
mid-50s.   Photo: D Stone

The famous Church traverse at Idwal. Members of the Sandstone CC, 1952. L to R: Ned
Cordery, Des Entwistle, Brian Schuster. Climbers have been 'buildering' like this since the
earliest days of rock-climbing in Britain.   Photo: D Stone

and this has been borne out for me by the misfortunes that have befallen many of my climbing friends over the years, with over 50 of them killed, and others badly injured. But an equally terrible fate awaited another climber of my acquaintance from the same era, whom I will call 'Z'. His story contains a message for outdoor enthusiasts everywhere. He appeared on the scene from the Manchester area in the late fifties, and he was fairly burning up the hard routes. The last time I ever saw him on rock was at Froggat Edge in 1960, when he was leading *The Great Crack*, a very hard lead for the period. He disappeared from the action shortly afterwards, and I must confess that I had forgotten about his existence. The next time I did meet him, however, was to be in entirely different circumstances – so different that I did not recognise him. It was almost a decade later, towards the end of the sixties. I was visiting the top security wing of Wakefield Prison to give a talk to the 'lifers', and a trustee was projecting some transparencies for me. After I had finished my talk I approached him to thank him for his able work, when I got the feeling that he recognised me.

"I know you," he said, "I used to be a climber myself." I looked hard at him for a moment and, despite his prison uniform and the intervening years, I finally recognised him as the climber from Manchester. I was aware that my audience that night were all convicted murderers so it was with some trepidation that I asked him for the details of his crime. (Some prisoners will talk freely about their situation, others will not.)

"I married in the early sixties and had been out climbing one Sunday, but stopped off for a few bevs with the lads on the way home. You know how it is?" he confided, and then went on, "When I arrived home my wife started giving me some stick because we had stayed so late at the pub, and I lost my temper and lashed out. I didn't mean to do it, but I hit her, and she fell and banged her head and died."

"Oh dear," I commiserated. "What happened next?"

"I was found guilty of murder and I've been here for nearly five years," he responded.

"But why didn't you contact the police immediately it happened. You might have been ccharged with manslaughter?" I opined.

"I was in the police, I was a sergeant, but I tried to cover it up. I buried her body in the back garden and told the neighbours she had gone back to live with her mother. It was six months before anyone found out! Do you know, I'd give anything to be able to walk up and climb at Stanage again. I never realised just how good life was on the outside until I lost my liberty. You tell all those climbers out there just how lucky they are to be able to go out climbing every weekend!"

And as he was led away by a warder, I assured him that I would do just that.

Chapter Six

Porridge

I had always imagined Scotland as a remote, uncharted wilderness, as difficult to approach as The Magic Mountain, and my earliest visits did not disappoint my expectations. On one of these visits I travelled to Glasgow to meet Mick Noon and his friends of the Creag Dhu – Porridge, Sunshine and the Monster – and we then journeyed on to climb on The Cobbler with a group including John Cunningham, Bill Smith and Hamish MacInnes. We plodded up The Cobbler and, as it was misty and damp, spent the afternoon 'bouldering' in boots on the Narnain Boulder, where it quickly became obvious that John Cunningham was the outstanding performer of the group, and, like Dolphin, possessed great finger strength. There is no doubt now, with the benefit of hindsight, that Cunningham, Brown and Dolphin were, in 1951, the outstanding rock-climbing pioneers.

This was also a golden era for the Dhus, and on my journey with them I grew to appreciate fully the initiative of working-class climbers in escaping from their awful inner-city environment, which appeared then to be a sea of slums and saloon bars, terribly depressing to an incomer – but there was nothing depressed about my gregarious Glaswegian friends, who joked and sang all the way to Arrochar. Every Dhu sported a flat cap, and they looked like the original 'No Mean City' gang. Their accents were so thick that I could barely follow their conversations, but it soon became apparent that, when the Dhus took a dislike to anyone, it went deep, and in that era (like my own friends in the Bradford Lads) this dislike was directed towards the climbing establishment, which in Scotland then meant the SMC. However, they were not afraid of turning the joke on themselves, and I laughed until I cried at the misfortunes that had befallen them.

One which stuck in my mind was the occasion one winter's night, when two of the Dhus found a deer which had been killed by a vehicle on the Rannoch Moor. The next day they somehow managed to hitch-hike back to Glasgow with this prize hidden inside a sack, believing that the big hotels or restaurants in the city would fall over one another to buy it. However, they soon found, after a couple of visits to hotel kitchens, that venison was out of season, and that there was no interest in purchasing the carcase. This left them with the real problem of how to dispose of the body, for what they were doing was illegal, and would be seen as poaching if the police got involved.

The Creag Dhu on The Cobbler, 1951. Pat Walsh is second from left, back row, with John Cunningham third from left; Mick Noon is third from right, middle row, with Bill Smith in front.
Photo: C Vigano

Eventually, they solved their dilemma by sawing the animal up and putting the pieces into a suitcase, which they deposited, under a false name and address, in the left-luggage room of Glasgow's Central Station. Nothing further was heard about this matter for many weeks, by which time it was high summer with a heat wave. Eventually, the headlines in the *Glasgow Herald* proclaimed, 'Body found in suitcase in station's left-luggage'. It transpired that, because of the smell from the baggage, the attendants had called in the Health Inspector. He had quickly located the offending case, but had mistaken its contents as being human, and it took some days before the decomposed remains were identified as those of a deer.

During my stay on The Cobbler I climbed with Mick Noon. Solidly built, of medium height and with gingery hair, he never stopped laughing. When I had climbed with him earlier that year in North Wales, he had not particularly impressed me – he had failed on Brant when Alfie Beanland and I had succeeded – but on his own midden he showed climbing skills that were outstanding for their era. Mick's bubbling enthusiasm made light of the

On the Narnain Boulder with the North Peak of The Cobbler behind.   Photo: D Gray

rain and the wet rock – a lichenous mica-schist which is notoriously greasy when wet – and we climbed four routes in boots. He led three routes, one of which was a 'Scottish' Very Severe, and would have defeated me without a tight rope. At the end of the day I was allowed to lead a mere Severe, *Cat Crawl*, which gave me a terrible fright for I had never experienced rock quite as slippery as on The Cobbler that day: as I moved out high above Mick, my feet shot off the rounded holds and I slid down a couple of feet, but somehow snatched a hand-hold just as I was about to shoot over the lip of an overhang. I was lucky for, climbing without protection, a ground fall would have been the result if I had not checked myself. MacInnes was laying siege to a large, unclimbed ceiling, which was undoubtedly the first major artificial climb in Britain. As befitted a man nick-named MacPiton, he was armed with every conceivable aid known to climbers at the time, many of which I had never seen before nor since. Despite a generous offer from one of his aides (known to the Dhus as 'Gnomies') to accompany them on what would be "the most important ascent in the history of The Cobbler, nay, British mountaineering," I said goodbye, and set forth to hitch-hike to Glencoe to meet Neville Drasdo.

At Cameron's Barn, 1951. L to R: Harold   Harold and Neville Drasdo climbing *Red*
Drasdo, Neville Drasdo, Tom Ransley.   *Slab*, Rannoch Wall, 1951. (The halo
                               Photo: T Ransley   encloses the climbers.)   Photo: T Ransley

Neville, his older brother, Harold and one of their climbing partners, Mike Dixon, were great enthusiasts for Scotland, and had convinced me that climbing north of the border was superior to anything in the Lakes or Wales. Mike Dixon had begun climbing at Ilkley and, like many others from that era, was a mite eccentric. Harold Drasdo who, with the demise of Alfie Beanland, is quite the best raconteur I know from that period, tells the story of how, on the first occasion that Mike came to his parents' home, he was sent to the local fish and chip shop for their evening meal. On returning with his precious cargo stuck down his jumper, he insisted on reciting a poem he had written before he would hand it over to Harold's amazed parents. I suppose this is what is known as a captive audience? His saga was so long that, by the time they managed to get their teeth into their cod and chips, they were cold!

In Glencoe, we stayed in Cameron's Barn, situated up in the Pass on the edge of the Inverness road. It was occupied by all sorts of odd characters besides climbers, and on my first night there, snuggling into the straw, I was awakened in the middle of the night by an old tramp, who had been sharing our lodgings, staggering out of the door declaring, "It's tae cauld fur me ... it's tae cauld fur me!" as he set off to seek warmth and shelter further down the Glen.

We were nothing if not ambitious in our plans and, after ascending *Agag's Groove* and a Very Severe which yielded easily to gritstone hand-jamming, we had a hard time in ascending *Red Slab* – all of these routes being on the Rannoch Wall of the Buachaille Etive Mor. This latter route proved so difficult that we nearly had to retreat, and as it was graded 'Severe in rubbers', the experience only helped to reinforce my opinion that Scottish climbing and climbers were more odd than those in other areas of the country.

Probably the hardest climb in Glencoe in 1951 was *Gallows Route* on the Buachaille, a route pioneered by John Cunningham in 1947, which had not then had a second ascent. (This was achieved by Whillans a short while later.) Neville, who was a few years older than me and a very gifted climber, decided we should cap our other successes by attempting this climb for the glory of the fatherland. I climbed up and belayed him from a pedestal at the start of a traverse, which leads leftwards across a steep wall to gain entrance into a groove line in the rock-face. This traverse is the crux of the climb, as I was to discover when climbing the route some years later. Neville set forth across the wall and, surprisingly, managed the manoeuvre withouuuuut too many problems, but then he stuck in the final groove above and, due to the lack of protection, for he had nothing between himself and me, he lost confidence. There was a rumour current amongst the Dhus at that time that the climb might not be possible after a key hold had broken off in the hands of Cunningham's second, causing him to fall. Neville managed to climb back down to the traverse line, but found he could not reverse it, and there he stuck, under a roof at the bottom of the groove, unable to move other than to shift his weight from one foot to the other, and similarly exercise his hands. Minutes slipped away as he marked time in that strenuous position. The impasse developed into an hour, then two, and that he managed to hang there so long is amazing. The shadows were lengthening, there were no other climbers about, and our situation was becoming serious, for we were, in a word, 'cragfast'.

Finally, I managed to flick our single, full-weight rope over a flake, and Neville decided that it was shit or bust. He implored me to take the rope in with every inch he made back across the traverse, convinced that he would fall. I was smaller than he and of much less bulk, but promised to do my best to get the rope in. With this assurance, in desperation, he set out, grabbing wildly, crab-like, climbing back across the wall. It is surprising how little in the way of contact you need in order to stay on the rock-face and, despite being out of control, Neville somehow managed to claw his way back to me without falling. As I grabbed him and pulled him onto my stance, our relief was so great that we both began cheering!

Because of Mike Dixon's influence, later that year I set out from Leeds to hitch-hike to Skye. The year before, Mike had spent all of his school holidays there and had made several first ascents, including the impressive *Crack of Dawn*, in the company of an Aberdonian climber, Bill Brooker. It was a long journey of several days, but I had plenty of time, thanks to school holidays. My route took in Loch Ailort and Morar, and on the way home I visited Kintail, Loch Ness and the Great Glen. The north-west could not fail to impress anyone with the gift of sight, but it was the characters I met on the road that enthralled me. I was well prepared, having read Alastair Borthwick's *Always a Little Further*, which is about the working-class climberrs and outdoor people of Scotland in the terrible depression years of the 1930s, and which remains for me the outstanding book of its genre – perhaps a Scottish equivalent of Kerouac's *On the Road*. I met tramps and hawkers, tinkers and gypsies, and even the long-gone berry-pickers. It was educative, to say the least, for my fifteen-year-old mind. One gentleman of the road (an old Dhu) took me poaching in a private loch above Mallaig, where we nearly got caught. We escaped with our spoils and the best part, as in so many of the Creag Dhu stories, was in lighting the fire and cooking the catch – fish never tasted better.

When I arrived on Skye, the weather was atrocious, but in Glen Brittle we had a portion of the MacRae's barn in which to shelter. This was above the cattle byres and was a single, long, dark room with a wooden floor. In spite of the rain I managed to climb a respectable number of routes along with Billy Boston and Ernie Leach of the Bradford Lads, Mike Dixon, plus the Aberdonians, Bill Brooker and Tom Patey; the latter pair even managed the traverse of the Cuillin Ridge. I did not realise at the time how significant this meeting was, for Tom was later to become a great friend, with whom I shared many eventful days. He was then a medical student in Aberdeen, but it was obvious that he intended greater things, and it was not surprising that he later went on to become a potent force in Scottish climbing circles, and also to make impressive first ascents in the Alps and Himalaya. However, at this first meeting, what impressed me most were his varied talents – his thoughtful wit, his musical abilities and his interesting stories. Amazingly, he had already heard 'the legend of Joe Brown', and he had a wonderful story about meeting a young Mancunian in a Cairngorms bothy earlier that year, who had enthralled the members of the Aberdeen University Lairig Club with tales of Joe's derring-do: "E's incredible... like a yuman spider! 'E doan't need any 'and 'olds. 'E uses suction, faith and friction!"

At the end of our stay the locals in Glen Brittle organised a ceilidh to celebrate the getting-in of the harvest. God knows how they had done this, for in the month I was there we had only one really fine day. The ceilidh was held in the MacRae's home and we were all invited. This, for me, was the outstanding event of the holiday, for although I had attended several such evenings at the home of relatives in Liverpool, it was my first time at a Highland gathering. I was impressed when Tom, during an interval, took over and played a piano, and I learned from him later that it had been a toss-up as to whether he would study music or concentrate on medicine. Over the next few years, Scotland became a must at Easter, first with the Bradford Lads, then in the bosom of the Rock and Ice. On these excursions I learned by hard experience that the scale and isolation of the mountains combine to give any winter outing in Scotland a spice and attraction lacking in summer crag or cliff climbing, and put the former activity into the realms of greater mountaineering.

The Ram and I had an eventful journey and stay in Scotland during the winter of 1956. We travelled from Leeds by train, but missed our connection north and had to spend some time waiting in Glasgow's Central Station. We were dressed in balaclavas, heavy jackets, boots, scarves and breeches against the fierce cold. While wandering aimlessly around the streets outside the station, trying to keep warm and just killing time, we were seized upon by a crowd of Glaswegians, very much the worse for drink. Explain as we might, they were convinced that we were Hungarians, escaped from the recent uprisings in Budapest. They insisted on buying us a heap of hot meat pies in the station buffet – quite the best in Britain at that date – and, after arguing with them for a while, I said to The Ram,

"For God's sake, agree we are Hungarians, or we'll never catch our train to Fort William," so heated had the argument become amongst our hosts about the recent events in our supposed country. Finally, accompanied by a lot of cursing and swearing and 'Ach aye's', we were allowed to board the Mallaig train, bolstered by the many expressions of regret from the Jocks that they personally had not been able to come over to Magyarland and lend a hand with the fighting.

For me there was something magic, then, about visiting Glasgow, and I remember as a boy hearing my father's stories about the fate of comedians

L to R: Sandy Crawford, Pat Walsh, Charlie Vigano beneath Clogwyn y Grochan in
1955.   Photo: C Vigano

and entertainers he had known, who had appeared at its famous Empire,
known as 'The Comics' Graveyard'. Every Glaswegian is his own
entertainer, his own natural comedian, and nowhere have I met people so
unconsciously funny – even more so than the Scouses. They have no need of
professionals, and thus find most such shows contrived.

Years later, when I worked in the Anderston district of the city, most days
I met someone with a very funny anecdote to tell. An illustration of this
unconscious element comes from my first meeting with Ian Nicholson in
Glasgow. His huge frame was clad in a very sharp suit, and, taking me to be
from Bradford, he said, "Aye, Bradford! It's a great place, mon!" This rather
surprised me, for I had never heard anyone enthuse so warmly about the
charms of the wool city. I timidly enquired, "Aye, I suppose it is, but why do
you think so?"

"Because, mon, Bradford has the best jumble sales in the country, Ye see
this suit I have on? Bought it at a jumble sale in Bradford for ten shillings."
That ended the conversation, for I did not dare ask what Big Ian had been
doing at a jumble sale in Bradford – the mind boggled!

The Rock and Ice were privileged to have two Scottish climbers in their
midst, in the persons of Pat Walsh and Charlie Vigano of the Creag Dhu,
who had moved south from Glasgow to Manchester to find work, and to take

part in the climbing activities of the club. Pat Walsh was, without doubt, one of the very best Scottish rock-climbers of the 1950s; a man of medium height, with a wonderful sense of the ridiculous and a most generous personality. He was physically very strong and was also one of the wildest men if provoked. On occasion, even Don Whillans was known to walk away, overwhelmed, and leave Pat to sort out as best he could the odds he had challenged in some bar or dance hall.

Pat was with us on one weekend's climbing on Hen Cloud. We were staying in a nearby barn (in which Ray Greenall contracted Bell's Facial Paralysis, on a separate occasion) and, after cooking up, we wandered down to The Rock, our regular Saturday night pub. A shock awaited us, however, for in our absence, climbing further afield over the summer, it had been transformed from a sleepy, rural public house into a tarted-up monstrosity full of gin-and-vodka types from Leek, Stoke and Stafford, their Jaguars parked in a newly created carpark. On entering the pub we noted a huge log fire at the end of the lounge in a recently constructed stone fireplace. It being cold outside, we sat as near to this as we could. This obviously displeased the nouveau riche clientele, judging by the looks that passed among them. In a situation like this, something had to happen, even more so when Pat overheard some rude remarks about us at the bar. This led to some kind of altercation with the landlord, and it was obvious to the rest of us, when Pat returned with our drinks, that the temperature was rising fast. For a while we continued to sit quietly amongst our unfriendly fellow customers, while they repeated, within our hearing, their rude observations, even so far as to suggest that we should not be allowed in the lounge, dressed as we were. This really annoyed us, for several of us present had been good customers at this hostelry for years. Suddenly, Pat stood up and said, "Would yae like to see an old Scottish custom, boys?" The rest of us, feeling a little perplexed, did not know how to reply, but Vin Betts, being a South Yorkshireman and a bit slow on the uptake, said, "Yeah. Show us your custom, Pat." At this command, Walsh calmly walked up to the fire and, to our utter astonishment, and without any warning, he unfastened his pants and began relieving himself on the fire! The room naturally began to fill up with steam and smoke, and it was obvious that the gin-and-vodka types were as gobsmacked as we were – they simply stood by in disgusted amazement. After he had finished, Pat calmly returned into our midst, sat back down as if his actions had been the most natural thing in the world, and simply continued sipping his pint with a genial smile on his lips.

"Bloody hell, Pat, that's a great custom," decided Vin Betts, and he strode up to the fireplace and began to repeat Pat's act. Unknown to him, Walsh dashed into the snug and grabbed the landlady's attention with the words, "This is a disgraceful place, there's a man relieving himself on the fire in your lounge!"

The woman came rushing into the room and it was obvious that, initially, she also could not believe her eyes. But, on recovering her composure, she decided on strong action, for we had been there many times in the past, and she doubtless knew who we were and that we were all together.

"Out! ... Out!" she screamed at us all. "And don't you ever come back. You're banned forever. You included," she decided, pointing a wagging finger at Pat, while all the bourgeoisie echoed their approval, standing at a safe distance and murmuring comments like, "Damned Manchester teddy boys," and, "They need horse-whipping, the lot of them!"

"I was only trying to help, missus," Pat reproached her.

"Get out, get out, before I fetch the police!" And so out we went with heads held high, but banned from The Rock pub.

Pat's arrival in Manchester gave added impetus to our activities in Scotland. He had been the first to realise the potential of Slime Wall on Buachaille Etive Mor, and his routes, such as *Bludgers*, *Revelation* and *Nightmare Traverse* were major breakthroughs. Morty, Ron Cummaford and I repeated these routes in 1958, but Patsy's descriptions of his climbs left us all at sea and we enjoyed a minor epic on *Nightmare Traverse*, strung out across one of the steepest pieces of rock in the country, totally lost as to the line to be followed. Patsy was noted for being vague about route detail and often he just climbed what appeared before him; this may have been partly due to his poor eyesight, for he wore glasses with lenses like jam-jar bottoms, but was just as likely due to the strength and superb ability that allowed him to climb almost anywhere. This phenomenal ability was illustrated in 1959 when Patsy, believing he was ascending *Sheaf* on Cloggy, went off route and climbed instead what became one of the main pitches of *The West Buttress Eliminate*, now known as *Walsh's Groove*. When he climbed this 'variation' he was with Charlie Vigano; Harry Smith and I were on an adjacent route, where we could hear but not see them. This new pitch was well over a hundred feet in length, continuously difficult and, in that era, totally unprotected. Pat still believed he was on *Sheaf*, a climb which is at least two grades easier, and we could hear him calling down to his second from high up the groove, "Aye, Charlie, those auld climbers could really climb!"

I experienced a similar incident with him that same year, when we made the third ascent of Cloggy's *Bloody Slab*. After he had climbed some way up the first pitch, which is the hardest on the climb, his glasses fell off and, half-blind from then on, he climbed more by feel than sight. He actually made a variation on this occasion that was slightly easier than the original line! Another such occurrence happened when we were climbing *White Slab* on the Black Cliff that same year. After I had led the initial entrance pitch, which is followed by an easy crack to gain the stance of Linnell's Leap, before the first serious slab pitch begins, Patsy wandered off route over to our left. Getting back across to the proper stance made the rest of the climb seem relatively simple. With Walsh you could never predict where you might end up, only that you would have a good time getting there. He was immensely powerful, but his jam-jar-bottom glasses gave him an air of studied innocence that many a brash young thug was to find out hid the real Patsy – a tremendous sight when he exploded into physical action.

The first time I saw him in action was at the Ambleside dance on a summer's weekend in 1958. Morty, Patsy and I had gone along there on the Saturday evening and, whilst Walsh was away at the bar, my companion and I sat watching the dancers, eyeing up the frippet. This was in the early days of rock and roll, and there was a couple on the floor boogying away to 'Rock Around the Clock'. The guy in particular was a real groover, a big farm lad who was bopping around as if he had ten thousand volts running through his body. But a few moments later he was to move even quicker. A lighted cigarette butt was thrown by one of the crowd behind Morty and me. It winged its way over the dance floor and fell down the back of the farmhand bopper's open-necked shirt. Now his gyrations were simply frantic as he jumped around, trying to stop himself being burnt by the offending tab-end. His antics made me laugh, but poor Mortimer was in hysterics, and when the rocker swung around, after finally removing the burning fag from his shirt, there was my companion, gesticulating to me at the fellow's predicament, and beside himself with mirth. This was too much for the farm boy and he ran at Mortimer, fist raised, and was just about to hit him when there was a blur of movement from behind us as Walsh returned from the bar. He dropped his drinks onto a table and then, 'wham!' the rocker never knew what hit him as he landed on the floor with a bump. The chap was not alone, and as Patsy turned around to face them, three other would-be assailants closed in on him. But then they thought better of it, for the Glaswegian looked as menacing as anyone I have ever seen. However, we were followed by a bout of name-calling as we made a hasty departure – and as we did so we were told by the organisers never to darken their doorsteps again.

Patsy was a Creag Dhu to his soul, and with him I camped at Jacksonville,

'Jacksonville' in 1953.   Photo: C Vigano   Bill Smith leading the first ascent of the
                                                 Direct Start to *Engineer's Crack* on Buachaille
                                                 Etive Mor in 1952.   Photo: C Vigano

the club's famous howff, under Buachaille Etive Mor in the spring of 1959.
We had come north especially to repeat *Carnivore* on Creag a' Bhancair, an
impressive cliff situated on the lower flanks of the Buachaille, which had
been pioneered in 1958 by two club members, John Cunningham and Mick
Noon. Before their success, Don Whillans had actually been as far as the
foot of the overhanging crack situated on the traverse of Pitch Four, by
which position the hardest climbing is done; but he had been trying to exit
straight up the crack, and had not been willing to continue traversing, which
is how the problem was eventually solved. Inevitably, The Villain returned
and climbed the crack, producing a Direct Finish which is harder than the
rest of *Carnivore*. During our stay at Jacksonville we were to meet many Dhu
legends, including Jackson himself. I had often wondered if the stories of
pre-war poaching and living off the land were factual, but once I had met
some of the characters from the 1930s and 40s, who could speak with
authority, I realised that, like all the legends, they were true. By 1959 the
poaching had become very sophisticated and could entail damming the
stream and dynamiting it!

Patsy had a U.S. Army two-man bivouac tent. These were made from the
thickest canvas I have ever seen, weighed a ton and buttoned at both ends,
but did not have a sewn-in groundsheet and were just like an envelope. Once

inside you had no idea if it was day or night outside, so impenetrable was the material. You could buy them from any respectable ex-WD store in the '50s for a very small sum of money indeed. They were incredibly durable, waterproof and ideal for camping in Scotland, and for some reason they even kept the midges at bay. Inside, with a primus roaring under a catering-size bean can full of water, with a wire for a handle (Patsy did not believe in wasting money on manufactured billies) even those flying pests retreated and gave you peace.

As we had no idea of the time, and had stayed late in the Kingshouse Hotel the night before, our start for *Carnivore* was a late one. If you climbed with Patsy it was at least as important to get to the pub in good time as it was to get on the rock. I can imagine he would have something to say about the trend for some of today's rock athletes to avoid the former – total incredulity would be an apt description. Everything went well with our ascent of *Carnivore* until the traverse of Pitch Four. This is set in a very impressive position under an overhang, and one had to make a step down, followed by a semi-hand traverse for dozens of feet across the wall, using a crack line under the roof for the hands. I watched anxiously as Pat led across this and was surprised to see, part way across, a piton stuck up in the ceiling above the traverse and, suspended from this, a sling with a piton hammer hanging from its end. We learnt later that this marked the point where Jimmy Marshall had fallen off and been forced to retreat a few weeks earlier. Pat clipped into the piton and then moved on, placing in all about five runners in a hundred feet before he reached the end of the pitch. He was a very bold leader, and five points of protection on one section of a route meant that by his standards it was a well-protected climb. I set forth and was doing alright until I reached Marshall's piton, when I realised that the rope was jammed at a chockstone runner Pat had placed in the crack further on. Panic set in, for I could now see that the rope was not being taken in, and so I hung a sling on the peg and pulled and tugged at our single hawser-laid rope until it was clear. Once this was done, and still in contact with the rock, I unclipped myself from the sling; but then, as an afterthought, decided to hang on the piton with the rope clipped in direct, while I adjusted the gear I was carrying. This left me in a very impressive position, hanging clear above hundreds of feet of space. I wondered to myself what would happen if one fell from this traverse, for below were some more overhangs. A few moments later I was to find out.

"Hold me," I shouted to Pat. The rope went tight round my waist, and all seemed well as I put my weight back onto the piton – one that did not inspire total confidence, for it protruded far out of its crack. Then, "Christ!" I was falling and down I shot for about twenty feet. Though I thought I had the rope tight between Patsy and myself, there had been more slack rope jammed at the chockstone than I had realised and my weight had finally freed it.

"Bloody hell!" I was being strangled, hanging from the rope around my waist and ribs, totally clear of any point of contact with the rock-face, and I shouted to Patsy to pull me in. Then, panic! What if he pulled so hard that the peg came out? The next point of protection, the chockstone, was dozens of feet away, and I would fall another distance ... if it held! In desperation, I started to climb up the rope. Those who have never climbed a thin, nylon rope will not appreciate how far twenty feet in such circumstances can seem, but for me it felt like hundreds. Hand over hand I pulled, and just as I was about to flake out, I reached the piton – but then I had another panic, for I could not take my hands off the rope in order for Pat to take it in and for me to clip into the peg. Finally I managed to grab a hold in the crack, retreat a little way along the traverse to some reasonable footholds, and get back into some kind of climbing order. Once I had started along the traverse again, the lack of protection, my hurting hands and the impressive position made the rest of the climb seem desperate, and I fought my way from hold to hold, several times almost falling again. Finally I reached Patsy and safety, to find him curled up in a sleepy hollow amongst the bilberries, sunbathing with his shirt off. After that experience I could not even lead the last easy pitch up a line of gently-angled slabs and Patsy almost had to haul me up these with my hands weakened and painful from climbing the rope. When we returned home I remember meeting Joe Brown and telling him that *Carnivore* was the hardest route I had ever done. I had forgotten, however, that he and Whillans had been some way up the crag during the Rock and Ice Easter bus trip of 1952, and he looked at me with a quizzical grin for a moment and then declared, "You must have been off form! That crag's full of big jugs."

Patsy, like Whillans, for some reason seemed to attract trouble. He was actually much less aggressive than Don, but there was the same un-compromising streak in him. Although, when climbing, he seemed happy enough bumbling up a classic easy route, he would never back down from a physical challenge. The stories are numerous, from the Doctor Barbara Moore incident to the alcohol in the teapot event. The first was during a run-in with a group of Manchester Teddy Boys near Deansgate in the centre of the city, when a climbing acquaintance of ours had been threatened and Walsh fortuitously arrived on the scene to save him from a potentially terrible fate, as he was heavily outnumbered. Patsy handed his jacket to this fellow-climber while he went round the corner to settle their differences with the Teddy Boys on a piece of waste land. However, as he reached the battle site, the police arrived and the rest of the belligerents departed at the run – but the cops managed to arrest Walsh.

"What are you doing in the middle of Manchester, late at night, in the freezing cold without your coat?" demanded the officer in charge.

"I am on a sponsored walk, officer, just like Doctor Barbara Moore!" Patsy insisted. Doctor B. was an old lady who was walking all over the place at the time, insisting that the whole nation should do the same to improve their health. Some said she was dotty, others plain crazy, but she was a phenomenal walker, despite her advanced years: having warmed up on the John o'Groats to Land's End Walk, she had progressed to even longer trogs; as can be imagined, the media loved her dearly. By the date of this incident there were literally dozens of people walking here, there and everywhere, emulating the good Doctor, at all hours of the day and night; and so the police, not totally convinced, but lacking any real evidence of a crime, let Patsy go. And then he did have to walk home to Whalley Range, for the bystander had still got his coat containing his wallet.

The alcohol in the teapot saga started out as a joke, but ended up for real. One of the Rock and Ice worked in a laboratory and had brought a winchester full of alcohol to a party, intending it to be consumed watered down with orange juice, blackcurrant and other soft drinks. But Patsy jokingly challenged Ron Cummaford to drink some of the alcohol neat, and so Ron poured an amount of the liquid into a teapot and the pair of them, very merry by this time, sat eyeing this on the kitchen table, daring each other to drink it, while the rest of us party-goers looked on with incredulity. No action seemed likely and we expected that the two contestants would back down until Ron apparently poured out a cupful and drank it. Unknown to Patsy, Cummaford had a second cup full of water hidden under the table and it was this he had substituted with sleight of hand and drunk. Walsh, not willing to ignore such a challenge, filled a tumbler with pure alcohol from the teapot, and before anyone of us could warn him, and much to everyone's consternation, he downed it in a 'oner'. A few minutes later this took effect, and Patsy passed out.

The boys, in a panic, thinking that Walsh might die, decided to take him home to his flat, strapped with slings onto the back of a motor-bike, and contacted a friendly doctor to meet them there, in order to render immediate medical assistance. This journey required someone to ride alongside Patsy and hold him upright with one hand – this job fell to Whillans. Everything went well until they reached a traffic light turning to red; the driver with Walsh on the pillion kept going, while Whillans braked. Don told me that it was one of the funniest sights he had ever seen in his life, for Patsy remained with his legs strapped to the bike, while his trunk flopped backwards, leaving his head down by the back wheel. "Just like a circus stuntman!" Whillans declared.

It was three days before Patsy recovered properly, and on the weekend after this, when he came to a club meet at Edale, he had one half-pint of beer on the Saturday night and was instantly merry from its effects.

The 1950s marked the beginning of the end of easy conversation in climbing cafés and pubs the length of the land, for slowly, as the decade progressed, more and more of these establishments fitted juke-boxes. I well remember our incredulity on turning up in Tommies Café in Otley one Sunday night in 1953 to find that they had fitted such a machine, and the hopelessness of trying to plan a forthcoming holiday to North Wales against the noise of Kay Starr singing 'The Wheel of Fortune' again and again and again. When such machines were first installed, their owners believed that you had to play them at high volume, and it was almost impossible to hear yourself speak above the noise. It took a long while for such developments to reach the outposts of the Empire, but one Friday night Patsy arrived at the Salutation Hotel, our usual meeting place in Ambleside, to find that it, too, had succumbed to noise pollution: and there in the bar was a gleaming monster Wurlitzer, and you could not hear yourself breathe, let alone speak.

There was a young Teddy Boy behind the bar, obviously imported from somewhere to the south, and Patsy politely said to him as he bought a pint, "Will ye nae turn down the box ... we cannae hear ourselves speak?"

"Fuck off, mate!" replied the Ted rudely.

"I'll gae ye five minutes tae turn it down," Patsy warned him, noting, as he did so, the time on his wrist watch. The atmosphere, as reported by those sharing Patsy's table, became electric, for obviously the youth had no idea as to the possibilities of what might happen, and he even had the stupidity to turn the monster up louder still. Patsy had driven north on his motor-bike and was wearing a pair of heavy climbing boots. He sat there, sipping his drink, relaxed and looking studious behind his spectacles, and those who did not know him could not have guessed what would happen next. At precisely five minutes from the time he gave his warning, Patsy stood up, stretched himself, then sprang into action. He ran across the room and 'Wham!' he kicked the juke-box two or three times so hard with his right boot that it exploded with a bang ... after which there was silence.

"Noo, that's better!" he declared, and quietly returned to finish his pint while all hell broke loose around him.

It took me quite a while to understand the climbing scene in Scotland, and it was not until I went to live there in the mid-60s that I truly appreciated the rivalries that existed between climbers from different parts of the country. I had, however, noted how keen was the satisfaction with which Patsy had handed back Jimmy Marshall his piton hammer after our ascent of *Carnivore*. (Jimmy was soon back on the climb and completed the route.) Competition between the Edinburgh and Glasgow-based climbers for first ascents paralleled my own experience in the south between the Lancastrian and Yorkshire groups. I am all for such friendly parochialism, but I do abhor chauvinism, English or Scottish.

Perhaps I can best illustrate what I mean by relating an incident when Dougal Haston, Robin Smith, Joe Brown and I were at Chamonix together in 1960. The weather had been terrible but we were determined to climb. The Scots, Dougal and Robin, wished to try a new route on the West Face of the Drus (later climbed by Royal Robins), Brown and I the then unclimbed South Face of Fou. We agreed to toss for it and I watched with concealed amusement while Brown produced his famous penny. He tossed it and, of course, won. We walked up to the Envers des Aiguilles hut to spend the night there before attempting the climb – this walk went more like a race. The last section of the route lay up slabs covered in powder snow, which was decidedly dangerous, and, though I would have liked a rope, I did not dare admit it, biting my lip for the honour of The White Rose. Joe and I had been in the Dolomites and were very fit after completing several major routes, but try as we might, we could not get in front of Robin. It was obvious that he would have died sooner than let us beat him to the hut, and so we grimly hung on to him as we ploughed along the last level section to the refuge, almost four abreast. No quarter was given, and so, sweating and puffing, we came towards the building together, staggering along as best our heavy packs allowed. Then Robin had a brain-wave – he started to sing, and try as we might, Brown and I could not match him in this, for we just did not have sufficient puff left. And so he finished the moral victor, whilst we reassured ourselves that whilst the Scots (Robin and Dougal) might be braver and stronger, we English (Joe and I) were more cunning, and thus everyone was happy. In the end we all fell around laughing at our combined stupidity in setting forth at all, for when we finally reached the Envers des Aiguilles refuge, no one had been there for over a week, despite its being high season.

Conditions on the Aiguilles above our heads were more akin to mid-winter for they were plastered in a heavy coating of snow and ice. Looking across the Mer de Glace towards the Drus, it was a similar vision that greeted us on the rare occasions when the mists parted.

On a later occasion Robin Smith accused me of writing a load of bullshit and throwing in my hand with the establishment. This was when I became Hon. Secretary of the Alpine Climbing Group (ACG) in 1961. I replied, writing on a long length of paper, headed 'narrow paper width for writing to a narrow-minded Scotsman'. But he then outsmarted me by immediately joining the ACG – a most worthy fellow.

The Alpine Club took in the ACG when it needed active, youthful mountaineers to keep up its position of authority, just as the Scottish Mountaineering Club (SMC), Scotland's premier club, has done with successive generations of ginger groups north of the border: the Luibeg Clansmen, the Currie Boys and, inevitably, The Squirrels. The SMC is as much a part of the traditional establishment as any climbing club in England, and when I was principal guest one year at their Annual Dinner, I was astonished to discover that it was a men-only affair. I had with me a climber from England who sported long hair (then almost de rigeur amongst those under 30), and halfway through the dinner the top table, loaded with the current Office Bearers and ex-Presidents, almost had a collective heart attack when they look across the crowded dining room and saw what they took to be a woman, smuggled illegally into their midst!

In the early 1960s I climbed on several occasions with Dougal Haston, particulary after Robin Smith's death in the Pamir in 1962. We climbed in places as diverse as Ben Nevis, Almscliff and the Dolomites, and partly through knowing Dougal, and partly because of a girl-friend, I moved to Edinburgh in 1965.

This was during the hey-day of the Squirrels, a very active and talented group of climbers who endorsed my own experience of such clubs. They were a small, close-knit body with a minimum of organisation and they enjoyed all aspects of mountaineering, including its social activities. With them I enjoyed many good weekends in Glencoe, at Laggan and in the Cairngorms. The latter became a second home for me and I spent two winters living there and made many friends. This was in the early days of skiing development when it was still a small enough community for all the keen activists to know each other. On my first evening after taking up residence in Edinburgh, I had an adventure, for I met some of the Squirrels in the Castle Rock pub and, after several pints of heavy, we decided to go and climb on the forbidden Salisbury Crags. It was a harsh winter that year and the rocks were buried in snow, but with Brian Robertson and Ian McEacheran in the lead, on a beautiful moonlicht nicht, we sneaked our way into the park at Holyrood and headed for a route which in summer is graded Very Difficult. I recall that luckily I was wearing climbing boots, which I had donned to cross the icy streets of Edinburgh from my flat in Manor Place to reach the pub. But some of the other members of our team were not as well shod. However, I was also wearing a sheepskin jacket over a city suit and the limitations of these clothes soon became apparent once I started climbing. I eventually had to throw my expensive coat down into the snow at the base of the route before I could climb the crux, which is a pull over a small roof to gain a good ledge. Getting onto the latter proved to be more difficult than I had anticipated, and as I stood up in triumph I heard a distinct rip from the seat of the pants of my expensive suit. Somehow, despite our inebriation, we all ascended the climb in good order, and it was this climb more than any other which founded my friendship with Alastair 'Bugs' McKeith, for, despite his youth, he was absolutely buzzing with the experience. As we walked back to our vehicles, parked a discreet distance away, despite our companions' insistence on absolute silence (in order to avoid attracting the attention of any Park Ranger stupid enough to be wandering around looking for climbers at 11pm) 'Bugs' just could not contain himself, and was bubbling with talk of future intended ascents, of Nordwands and bivouacs. His enthusiasm was truly infectious.

It is surprising to me now that I remember details of only a handful of the climbs we did together in the Highlands, whilst I can recall quite vividly urban events in Edinburgh and Glasgow. For instance, the high tree near to Brian Robertson's house, which he pegged, and which was desperate to climb without etriers, just using the pitons to pull on. And then there were the trips to the Currie Walls, which Dougal Haston, Robin Smith, the Squirrels and many more climbers of that era, trained upon. There were also many parties and one classic was held in the old SMC club rooms in Edinburgh, when we rolled barrels of beer up through the cobbled High Street. Not even Auld Reekie, though, could match the revels held in Mary Stewart's house at Balmore outside Glasgow. Her gatherings had a truly international flavour, since she was an American climber and had contacts among that country's leading activists. On one memorable occasion John Harlin, Layton Kor and Gary Hemming were all present. The music and singing were also of a very high standard for, besides Tom Patey, we were often joined by professional folk musicians such as Alex Campbell and

Salisbury Crags, Edinburgh.   Photo: D Bathgate

Building the Squirrel's Dray in Glencoe, 1964. L to R: Doug Lang, Dave Bathgate, Brian
Robertson bending, farthest right Jim Brumfitt.   Photo: J Renny

The first Squirrel's dinner at the Kinshouse, 1963.   Photo: J Renny

Dougal Haston on the first winter ascent of   Dougal Haston on the *Buhlweg*, Rotwand, in
Gargoyle Wall, Ben Nevis, Feb. 1963.   the Dolomites, 1963.   Photo: D Gray
Photo: D Gray

Hamish Imlach, plus groups like the Incredible String Band.

I worked for a printing firm in Glasgow, but lived in Edinburgh across the road from Professor Graham Brown of Brenva fame. I had a roving commission throughout Scotland, for we had the contract not only for printing passes for the Cairngorm Chair Lift, but also for Aberdeen's bus tickets. On one occasion I even went to Ullapool to meet representatives of that Council, who had decided on a promotional brochure to attract tourists to their beautiful town. While there, I stayed with Betty and Tom Patey, for the latter was the local doctor and had the biggest practice (geographically) in Britain. When I stayed over in Glasgow, I used to go along to meet the Creag Dhu in a bar in West Nile Street, which actually boasted sawdust on its floor and spitoons in each corner of the room. I also mixed with members of the Langside MC, who had the use of one of the earliest UK climbing walls, situated in Langside College.

One of our regular meeting places in the Highlands was the Loch Laggan Inn, adjacent to Creag Meagaidh. Mine hosts were John and Margaret Small, and they revelled in the company of climbers. (John himself began to climb when over fifty years of age with Tom Patey.) They provided a free

Alastair McKeith on the first winter traverse of *Apolyon Ledge*, Creag Meagaidh.   Photo: D Gray

bothy for us to doss in at the side of the hotel. The ceilidhs held there at that time were outstanding, with both locals and climbers joining in vigourously. Unfortunately, the Inn was a wooden structure and caught fire. John was in the bath at the time, and escaped with only a bath towel wrapped around him to watch his Inn burn to the ground whilst awaiting the fire engine from Kingussie.

After this it was in the Cairngorms that the action was to be found, on the hill during the day and in the pubs at night. There were many wonderful characters around in Aviemore in the mid-60s, one of whom was Sandy, who had a shop at Loch Morlich. Sandy started climbing with another friend, Tom Murphy, and as young, impecunious lads, they had not been able to afford a rope. Tom used to tell the story of how they solved this problem by obtaining a long piece of piano wire, on which they proceeded to ascend the local classics, such as *Aladdin's Couloir*, until one day, whilst climbing in Coire an Lochan, he slipped and fell. Somehow Sandy managed to hold him and stop his fall, even though the piano wire cut into his hands. Tom swore that as his weight came fully onto the wire, it gave out a perfect 'G'!

In the winter of 1965, with Sandy, Eric Beard, Tom Murphy and George McLeod, I had the unusual experience of substituting for a professional ceilidh band at Tomintoul. Tom was a civil engineer and worked abroad, but

was home on a flying visit. One evening, after climbing in the Northern
Corries, we had retreated for a celebratory meal at the Rank Hotel at
Rothiemurchus, when the call came. A distraught lady organiser of the
annual ceilidh at the Tomintoul distillery phoned the hotel and pleaded with
George McLeod, a mountaineer who was also an accomplished musician, to
form a scratch band and come over immediately to replace the professional
band, who were hopelessly stuck in a snowdrift somewhere near Inverness.
Sandy agreed to try to drive us to Tomintoul in his car, despite there being a
blizzard howling outside, and we set forth, first to pick up our assorted
instruments from Glenmore and then to head up the Spey Valley for
Grantown and Tomintoul.

It was about ten p.m. when we finally arrived, after traversing roads made
treacherous by masses of fresh powder snow. We were greeted by the locals
as if we had just relieved Mafeking, for the only entertainment they had
managed up to that point had been from a little man called Fred, who
danced around playing the spoons, and in between drank copious amounts
of Tomintoul's best product. To say that this was liberally available is a half-
truth, for there was enough malt to have satisfied the whole of the SMC, and
poor old Fred had become so inebriated that he was reeling around the room
instead of dancing. After a swift dram to warm us up, we took over the task of
providing the music and entertainment. We soon organised a *Strip the
Willow*, then played the *Gay Gordons*, *McDonald's Rant* and many eightsome
reels. Then there were recitations by Beardie of items such as *Sonia Snell*,
The Battle of Hastings and *Albert in the Lion's Den*, and we finally hit our
audience with some good old rock and roll – Elvis, Little Richard and Adam
Faith. We received a good reception from the Highland audience, and thus,
in the early hours of the morning (a good ceilidh always sees in the dawn),
the evening came to a successful close. The lady organiser was incredibly
grateful to us for our efforts, and to thank us for our help she handed over
several bottles of the best Tomintoul malt.

"What about Fred?" she demanded, as we were leaving the hall to drive
back to Speyside. The little spoon player was curled up, fast asleep in a
corner. No one seemed to know where he had come from, nor where he was
going, only that he had suddenly appeared in their midst in their hour of
need and done his best to keep the party going.

"I think he cam frae Aviemore," volunteered one of the distillery workers.

"Aye, I'm sure I heard him say that," agreed another.

"Will ye nae tak him hame?" pleaded the lady organiser, "The poor wee
mon cannae stay in the distillery."

And so, reluctantly, we agreed to take him to Aviemore as we journeyed home to Glenmore.

He slept like a babe all the way back to Aviemore, not noticing the icy roads, nor even the terrible time poor Sandy endured at the wheel as another blizzard hit us. Finally, at six a.m., we arrived in the main street of the town, with the snow still falling.

"Oi, wake up, wake up!" we shook and punched Fred, and slowly he opened his eyes.

"Where am I?" he demanded, obviously in total confusion as he stared blearily through the car's windscreen.

"Aviemore!" we informed him.

"What the hell did ye bring me here for? I'm frae Aberdeen!" We still put him out into the snow and waved him goodbye... Perhaps he is even now entertaining the skiers with his spoons and dancing in one of the large Speyside hotels?

Nat Allen – 'catcher' at Black Rocks.   Photo: Gray coll.

Chapter Seven

Imbibing the Real Malt

On my first visit to the Cairngorms many years before, the access road ended at Rothiemurchus, but by 1965 the scene had altered out of all recognition; the skiing potential of the region had changed it from one of the most remote mountain districts in Britain to the centre of Scotland's winter sports. The road to the ski-lifts built high on Cairngorm itself gave quick access into the mountains and, although some climbers may deplore the invasion of a winter domain once solely theirs, one does not have to walk far to avoid the piste-bound downhill hordes. Often after a day's climbing in the winters of 1965 and 1966 Eric Beard and I used to ride down the piste of The White Lady on a large shovel, sitting two up at speeds that would have done credit to the Olympic Luge competitions. This action did not entirely endear us to the skiers, who claimed we damaged the piste.

During those two winter seasons there was a thriving night-scene in Carrbridge. Beardie had his sing-song two nights a week in the Carrbridge Hotel, but other nights we would meet in Karl Fuchs' place, Struan House, or at Jimmie Ross's hotel, The Rowanlea. Jimmie was one of the acknowledged masters of Highland fiddling, and his playing, often accompanied by Tom Patey on the accordion, was an unforgettable sound. Down the road in Aviemore there was the Saturday night dance in the centre, and one Saturday I went along there with a crowd of climbing friends, most of whom were single males, looking for female company. However, despite much posturing and chatting-up of the girls, we got absolutely nowhere, and it was obviously going to be just another of those failed Saturday nights. Late in the evening we were gathered around a table, commiserating with each other, when the most beautiful girl any of us had ever seen came over. However, the blonde gave us young blades not a glance, but seized on an old, staid, grey-haired, married man (his wife was at home, minding the children, south of the border), and asked, "Would you like to dance with me?"

Would he! And he did. He had that dance, and the next one, and the next one, and then he and Miss Right of 1966, after several affectionate hugs and a kiss, collected their coats and disappeared out to the carpark. Grey Locks did not return until the next morning, but many were the comments in his absence of what a lucky fellow he was. When he staggered into the doss, looking as if he had been up all night, he said not a word about his nocturnal activities. Then, a few months later, I ran across him at a boring club dinner in the Peak District, and we retired to the bar. We had a dram and then another and, with liquor loosening his tongue, he let slip that he was going to Inverness the following week to act as a witness in a criminal case.

"Inverness?" I gasped, smelling that I was onto something; and, after I had plied him with another double, he told me what had happened with Miss Right on that January night in Aviemore.

Once they had got outside into the carpark, she had become all lovey-dovey and asked if he would run her home in his car.

"No problem," said my gallant friend. "Where do you live?"

"Inverness!" she had replied, coyly.

"Bloody hell," thought Grey Locks, "it's a long way to Inverness, but it might be worth it." And so they set out for the capital of the north in his Sunbeam Talbot. They were burning up the A9 when out of the night appeared a line of police cars. 'Stop' lights flashed on, and one vehicle pulled in front and almost hit the Talbot, just like a Hollywood movie. "Get out of your car," came the dramatic command through a megaphone, and he and the girl did as they were told. The next moment Grey Locks found himself manhandled and handcuffed.

He spent most of the rest of the night being interrogated by the police, who, after a while, realised that he was not the professional accomplice of Miss Right 1966, who had made off with the takings of the Aviemore dance. On searching her, they found the missing money stuffed about her person, but mainly in her knickers. After he had finished his story, I promised not to tell the others the truth, and they have gone on believing that old Grey Locks is the possessor of an irresistible charm with the ladies, a reputation he boasts until this day in his own climbing club.

During my second winter in the Cairngorms, I was sometimes a member of the Rescue Team, while instructing at Glenmore Lodge. We would often be called out in the middle of the night, and usually, when this happened, the conditions were atrocious. The most difficult rescue that I took part in was when a male student from the Glasgow University MC fell while descending from Ben Macdui towards the Lairig Ghru, and was lying badly injured on a ledge on cliffs above the Pools of Dee. Fortunately, at Glenmore at the time we had a large survival course, made up of climbers, commandos, mountain rescue personnel and many others. The nearest we could get to the scene with a vehicle and an ambulance was Rothiemurchus Lodge, from where it was many miles to the ledge where the injured climber lay. A companion had stayed with the victim, and he signalled from the face with a head-torch as our advance party arrived below; otherwise we would never have found them. Half a dozen of our team had literally run through the night to that spot, as best as the dark and deep snow would allow, but when we got to the base of the cliff it was truly daunting to see how far up the casualty was from the valley floor. Climbing by head-torch, I cramponned and cut my way up to him, running out a light rope, from a huge drum, with which to pull up the MacInnes stretcher. Dr Gordon Waddell climbed up with me and, when we finally reached the casualty, we were alarmed to find that he had a fractured skull and other severe injuries. He was unconscious and, had he not been young and strong, he would probably have been dead from the cold, if not from his wounds. Gordon rendered what aid he could to the lad, and we put him in a sleeping bag to keep him warm. Then we decided to lower him immediately, even though we had only three of us to act as anchor men, for there was no time to bring anyone else up, and speed was of the essence if we were to save his life.

Pulling up the stretcher to the ledge was not so difficult. Lowering the stretcher with the casualty strapped in place down 800 feet on a thin hawser-laid rope was back-breaking work. Up to that moment the night had been as black as a bag and windy, but no snow had fallen. However, just as we were completing the lower, it began to fall in earnest.

As soon as the stretcher reached the valley floor, it was seized by a waiting group of climbers and the carry-out began. We had already arranged this before setting out from Rothiemurchus, and had formed teams of six who would carry the MacInnes about a half-mile each, for we had the amazing number of forty-two people strung out down the Lairig Ghru, ready and waiting in teams to take their turn at carrying the stretcher. The pass of the Lairig Ghru can be a grim place by day, but that night in a snowstorm it was a terrible wasteland, featureless and inhospitable.

Although climbing up to reach the casualty had been technically easy, descending the slope in a blizzard required extreme care and took a great deal of effort. By the time Gordon, the casualty's friend and I had descended to the foot of the cliffs, the first team was well on its way, struggling through the snow with its burden. We had with us a local shepherd, Peter, who knew the area of the Lairig Ghru as well as any man alive. He had led us unerringly to the Pools of Dee, and now, going back out to Rothiemurchus, he moved along almost at a trot just in front of the stretcher, picking the best route, never wasting a moment, and speeding up the process whenever the carriers were lagging by taking a hand at the head of the stretcher. It took

The Glenmore Lodge lorry of the 60s with Liam Carver.   Photo: D Gray

several hours of staggering along like this, changing the exhausted carrying teams every half hour, charging along through stream beds, falling down bankings, wading through snowdrifts, before we finally rushed up the last hill out of the Lairig to reach our destination just as it was getting light. It was a tremendous relief to see the ambulance with the casualty aboard speed off on its way to Inverness.

Everyone was exhausted, and climbed with relief into a waiting lorry to travel back to Glenmore, with thoughts of hot showers, a bed and warm blankets dominating our minds. However, the vehicle had been parked near the edge of the Lodge carpark, which is set above a sizeable drop. I clambered into the driver's seat, dog-tired, fearful that we might not have been in time and that the climber might die, wondering whether we could have reached him sooner and worrying about the length of time it had taken to get him out. As leader of the operation out on the hill these concerns were occupying my mind as I started up the engine, peered through the windscreen as the wipers started to remove the layer of snow, pushed the lever into gear and put my foot on the accelerator to move off. Then screams came from the rear as we shot backwards! I had put the lorry into reverse instead of forward gear and, as I slammed on the brakes, I only just stopped us from shooting out into space; in fact, the back wheels were right on the edge. I woke suddenly out of my torpor, for there were forty people clinging onto the back of the truck and any second we might all go over the drop. I realised that I had to act quickly, slammed the gear stick into first and put my foot hard down on the accelerator. We shot forward as if at the start of a Grand Prix race and nearly hit the side of the Lodge – but we were clear of the drop, to loud cheers of relief from my passengers. I have sometimes wondered what would have happened if we had gone over: it might have been a case of, "You've heard of the Glenmore disaster and the terrible price that was paid – one poor, dozy Yorkshireman was lost and forty men of the rescue brigade!" It really does not bear thinking about for too long.

It was even more of a relief later that day when the surgeon phoned from Inverness to say that the injured man would survive and should make a good recovery. They had been just in time to trepan his skull and relieve the pressure on his brain from internal bleeding. And so it did seem worthwhile, despite the near disaster.

In the light of present knowledge, it is surprising to recall that in the mid-60s we were only just beginning to realise the seriousness of avalanche danger in Scotland. Before this time, several of my climbing friends had had narrow escapes, but until the 60s we were misguided enough to consider the Highlands too small in scale to present real danger from avalanches. My own opinion was to change when, on an exercise in the winter of 1965, I was a volunteer 'casualty' and was buried in the snow when a blizzard suddenly reduced visibility to zero. Fortunately, Hamish MacInnes (a pioneer in the use of dogs for such work in Scotland) was on the scene with his specially trained Alsatian dogs. I had stupidly refused to take a two-way wireless under the snow with me, and I doubt whether I should have been found again, but for the dogs.

Being under snow is an eerie experience; you can breathe, as long as fine powder snow has not choked your lungs; but with six inches of snow on top of you, you are imprisoned as immovably as if you were set in concrete. The true severity of avalanches was bought home to us when Molly Porter – a member of the Rescue Team and a mountain guide who knew the area as well as anyone – and Ray Burnett from the Squirrels were carried down in a wind-slab avalanche that same winter. They were descending near Lurcher's Crag after a day's climbing in the Northern Corries. Molly escaped with a damaged leg, but Ray was severely injured. When we returned to the scene on the day after the avalanche, we were astonished at its scale: literally thousands of tons of snow had fallen over an area of a hundred yards or more.

Hamish MacInnes (bottom rt.) digging out Dennis Gray in 1967.   Photo: Gray coll.

Winter weather in the Cairngorms can be arctic and wind speeds can be
phenomenal. On one of my trips to this area, the wind on top of Cairngorm
was over 200 mph. In such winds it is impossible to move around. You
certainly cannot walk straight into them, and if caught out in the open the
only course is to go with the air-stream; it was only this fact that saved three
lives one winter's night in February, 1966.

Mary Stewart and two young climbers, members of one of our courses,
arrived on the plateau into such a wind, after completing a climb in Coire an
t-Sneachda. As they traversed off near the top of Coire Raibert, one of the
students needed to put on an extra pair of gloves against the wind-chill,
which was freezing his hands; but as he tried to take off his rucksack, it was
wrenched from him by a strong gust of wind and disappeared down the
slopes towards Loch Avon. They descended to retrieve the rucksack but,
once they had recovered it, they found that they could not climb back up
Coire Raibert, so strong had the wind become. So, in the gathering gloom,
they descended all the way to the loch and then followed its shoreline until

they could head off towards Strath Nethy. This is a very long way round to get back to Glenmore but, although the ground is boggy and tiring to walk on, it is usually sheltered and provides a safe way out of the Cairngorm massif and back into the Ryvoan Valley.

They staggered along in the Nethy, cursing and swearing as they fell down bog holes and crashed through ice into the stream. Just as it was getting dark, they came across an exhausted climber, collapsed at the side of the Nethy. Despite his youth, he had been unable to walk any further.

"My two friends have gone for help," he informed them. Mary was immediately concerned, for it was almost dark, and the man was young and badly equipped. She decided that they could not leave him there, out in the open, for the storm was increasing, and by the time his friends had got down to Glenmore, raised the alarm and the Rescue Team had returned, the youth might be dead. So, supported by Mary and her two companions, they got him to his feet and helped him along as best they could. Despite their own fatigue, they managed this for a long way until they found a second man collapsed in the stream bed – and he was unconscious.

It transpired that he was one of the two companions who had gone for help. Fortunately, this second casualty was not too far from the Bynack Stable – the bothy in the Nethy valley – so they put the unconscious man into a large polythene survival bag, then commenced dragging it through the snow, while continuing to help the first youth. After a great struggle they managed to reach the bothy, and inside found the third man. He, too, had collapsed, unable to go any further. Thus, without the fortuitous arrival of Mary Stewart and her two companions, at least two of that party might have died. Mary ran to Glenmore Lodge, alerted the rescue, and the two worst casualties were taken out by Landrover from Ryvoan bothy later that same night. All three recovered totally by the following day.

At that time, Mountain Rescue in Scotland was much more rudimentary than it is today, when teams such as that in Glencoe are as well equipped and organised as any. Also, they can call upon helicopters from the military much more freely than before, and the pilots have now developed great skill, and exhibit outstanding daring when helping with mountain rescues.

In the 1960s, the presiding spirit of Scottish mountain rescue was Ben Humble. He was a funny, wee gnome of a man, with a bald head and glasses. Everyone who climbed in the Cairngorms at that period knew and had the greatest affection for him. Despite his advanced years, his enthusiasm for the hills was undiminished, and his photographic books, such as *The Cuillin of Skye*, are still unsurpassed in their ability to capture the mood and history of climbing in Scotland. He had been a dentist in Glasgow but had become stone deaf and, as he used to tell us with a chuckle, he had had to stop practising when he could no longer hear his patients scream! He once came climbing with me in Coire an Lochan, but in a high wind he could not keep his balance, owing to his hearing difficulties and, as he kept falling over, we were forced to retreat.

Ben had a ghoulish sense of humour and you needed a strong stomach to attend his lecture on 'The History of Mountain Rescue in Scotland'. He would punctuate his commentary as he showed slides of dead bodies in many horrible, contorted positions, by shouting out at regular intervals, "When the Rescue Team reached them, there was blood everywhere!" I was at one of his lectures at Glenmore when one of the audience fainted and several others had to depart in a hurry, feeling queazy. Someone finally took such exception to Ben's delivery that they stole his box of transparencies.

The closest escape from a serious accident I ever saw in the Cairngorms was one day in February. I had led a party up *Aladdin's Mirror* and met Robin Ford from Aberdeen, who had just led an enormous man of about twenty stone up the easier Couloir route. Our climbs converged by the side of a large pinnacle, and my party of two students joined with Robin and his client in deciding to have lunch in that spot, sheltered as it was from the howling wind up on the plateau. The big man was, we soon appreciated, a wonderful story-teller, and whilst we ate our lunch, he told us joke after joke, which had the whole group laughing. One of these jokes entailed a demonstration, standing up with accompanying actions. He was in the middle of this performance when we suddenly realised that he was fast disappearing from view and had begun sliding upright, in an almost classic standing glissade. In an instant he was falling. Robin, who was tied to him and was still holding the rope in coils between them, stood up for a second, gobsmacked, obviously unable to believe his eyes; for the ledge the man had disappeared from was so large you would not have thought it possible to fall off. Then Ford sprang into action. He dived onto the slope to our left, pushed his axe in as far as it would go, and whipped the falling man's rope around it. Standing helplessly by, I expected that he would simply be pulled off and the ice-axe be wrenched from its placement; but no – amazingly, it held, and the huge man was stopped after falling almost thirty feet. One shudders to think what might have happened if the snow had been so soft that Robin could not have stuck his axe in and made such a quick belay.

A short while before I arrived in Edinburgh, Brian Robertson had almost free-climbed a short artificial rock-climb at Craig-y-Barns near

Brian Robertson on the Pentlands.
Photo: J Renny

Brian Robertson climbing on the sea cliffs at
Aberdour, 1965.   Photo: D Gray

Dunkeld, a crag now rich in association with Auld Reekie's climbers. This route is named *Rat Race*, and inevitably he more or less insisted that Bugs and I attempt to repeat his then hardest climb. Brian was one of the most enthusiastic climbers I have known. Short, stocky and fair-haired, as a boy he had fallen out of Raven's Gully in Glencoe and been badly injured. But this had only inspired him to try harder, and he was one of the great characters on the scene when I lived in Auld Reekie. He now lives in Colorado, and the last time I heard anything about him was when my old friend, Harold Drasdo, was visiting Boulder, looking for another friend of ours who now lives in that city. After journeying over 3000 miles, he knocked on the man's front door and was greeted by silence. A passing citizen noticed him and advised, "If you're looking for Gordon, he left on vacation yesterday for England."

"Damn!" Harold thought.

"If you're from Britain, why don't you go visit the crazy Scotsman? He lives just round the block, and he's building a full-size Spitfire in his basement! I'll take you there if you like," offered the helpful American. Harold was so intrigued, and his informant so insistent, that he agreed.

Interest turned to amazement when his knock was answered by Brian Robertson – and it turned out to be true, he was building a full-size Spitfire in his basement!

Craig-y-Barns is set among woods above the A9 Pitlochry road and, although it is a small cliff, it is very steep and covered in overhangs; *Rat Race* traverses below the biggest of these. After Bugs had led up to a ledge about 70 feet above the ground, I set out along the next pitch – the crux – climbing along underneath the ceiling. To gain this I had to pull on some in situ pitons, but once under the roofs I managed to free-climb the rest, using the pegs that Brian had placed for protection. I was just finishing the pitch when I heard from below a terrible squawking and squealing. I recognised Bugs's anxious voice shouting, "Aye! ... Get lost, will yae!" Once I had belayed and taken in his rope, he climbed up as if the hounds of hell were after him. "What's happening, who's after you?" I demanded. "It was an eagle, mon, it came straight at me. I thought it would take ma heed right aff!" On the way down after our climb we saw the bird in question, hovering over the cliff, only it was a buzzard, not an eagle. We must have disturbed it territorially, otherwise I cannot imagine it attacking anyone.

While living in Edinburgh I made good friends with many other Scottish climbers outside the Squirrels, including several of the Etchachan Club from Aberdeen, and in particular Jim McArtney. I first met him and several others from that club on Creag Meagaidh, and we became firm friends until his death on Ben Nevis in January, 1970. He was without doubt the strongest winter climber of his generation. In the winter of 1966/7 I visited the Granite City to lecture to the Etchachan Club on our Andean Expedition of the previous summer, when we had made the first ascent of Alpamayo's North Ridge. I was also the guest at their Annual Dinner, held that same weekend. The joke of the occasion was that Jim ended up by being my guest, since he had been dismissed from their members' list for sleeping where he should not, in company he should not have kept. But Jim was still the king, and after the dinner he organised the biggest carry-out I have ever seen (a good Scottish tradition). The kitty was £5, and it resulted in three van-loads of drink being carted round to his parents' home at two in the morning. The ensuing ceilidh still echoed as we left Aberdeen on the following night.

It was with the Aberdonians that one could enjoy most the real malt of Scottish climbing, and for me this was epitomised by climbing, with and socialising alongside, the doyen of their clan, Tom Patey. Anyone who has read his posthumously published book, *One Man's Mountains*, will not need any convincing of his unique wit and humour, but what is not really apparent

Jim McCartney climbing in the Polish Tatra, 1967.   Photo: D Gray

from this self-deprecating work is just what a climbing force Tom was. Truly, the worth of his achievements in mountaineering marks him out as one of the outstanding performers of his or any other generation. Tom was the most unlikely-looking Doctor I have yet come across, for he looked more like a boxer than a 'Dr Finlay'. Powerfully built, of medium height and with bushy dark hair, he had a face which looked as if it had been hewn from the stone of his native county. I have never seen anyone climb quite like him; he was ungainly and he used his knees when rock-climbing more than anybody I have climbed with; but he was truly effective in simply getting up climbs with speed, and, on mixed ground or easy grade rock or ice, he was a whirlwind of movement.

Spontaneity played a large part in his climbing activities, and he often made do with a minimum of equipment, enjoyed travelling light and would think nothing of climbing all day without a rest or a stop for food. He had built up an incredible bodily stamina over the years and he could manage on a minimum of sleep for days on end. It was nothing to him to play the

Tom Patey at the top of *The Red Wall*, Gogarth.   Photo D Gray

accordion at a ceilidh until the wee small hours, then set off up the hill for a major climb after snatching only two or three hours' rest. He loved to solo climb and with him I once completed 2000 feet of Severe-grade climbing in a day in Torridon. We carried a rope for emergencies only, and one sensed that it was the sheer joy of moving fast and safely up the cliff which he loved, for, despite his style, he was an exceedingly safe climber. As he pointed out, the habitual solo climber has to be competent, otherwise he will soon be dead.

We used to carry on a correspondence by sending each other postcards or application forms for membership of senior climbing clubs such as the SMC, the AC, the CC, filled in with what we felt were humorous comment. I would address these to 'My Lord Patey of the Isles', or 'Pom Tatey', and he would respond by addressing me as 'Dennis Gravy', or 'The Yorkshire Scot'. I can remember that in my joke c.v. for application to join the SMC, prepared by Tom, my prime qualification was that of being 'Joker at the Court of the Baron Brown'.

He needed to drive phenomenal distances each year in his medical practice, and had bought a Skoda in the early 1960s, when some glib salesman had convinced him that they were good cars. Then he had found that he was stuck beyond the Iron Curtain, for no other dealer would accept them in part exchange. On one occasion he was driving me in this vehicle from Ben Nevis to Bradford, where I had to give a lecture, and we were running behind schedule. It was a very dark night, and raining, but as I knew the road leading south extremely well, we devised a scheme to speed things up: we would use the classic O. G. Jones climbing grades for the bends. As we approached each one I would shout out 'Difficult', 'Severe' or 'Very Severe', and Tom, relying totally on my opinion, would either brake or push the car to its limits (which were not impressive). This worked like a charm and we rushed through Glasgow, over Beattock, on over Shap and then through Kendal. We seemed to have the operation totally under control until I was distracted by Tom who, whilst we were passing a road sign warning, 'Mud on the Road', suddenly exclaimed, "Blood on the Road", in a story about a particularly gruesome car crash to which he had been called earlier in the week near Ullapool. This happened as we came screaming up to the acute Z-bend of the bridge at Ingleton. With both of us in hysterics at this story, I managed to get out a 'Severe' as we roared into the bend, but should have shouted, 'Extreme'. Despite the gallant efforts of the good Doctor, our speed and line were too acute and the Skoda crashed ... and that put an end to our experiments with grading systems to assist drivers.

I was with Tom on another occasion in the 60s when he went to give a lecture to the AC in London. We had the usual excitement getting there in the Skoda, Tom doing a full change out of his climbing gear into his Doctor's grey suit, shirt, collar and tie as we roared through London's rush hour traffic. His shirt stuck as he was bringing it over his head, and we nearly hit a shiny new BMW. At the club we rang the door bell and this was answered by the indomitable Mrs Lewis, the long-serving housekeeper to the club. She could have doubled for 'Big Daddy', and sported a beard that many a male alpinist would have been proud of.

"What do you want?" she demanded. "To come in," replied the surprised Patey. "Are you members?" she then asked. "Yes we are," I interrupted. She looked hard at us for a moment, then decided, "We've had lots of your sort round here recently. You cannot be members... You're too young!" and she slammed the door in our faces.

"What an incredible woman!" observed Tom in stunned admiration, as we retreated across the road to the Audley Arms. We were finally rescued from the bar by the late Anthony Rawlinson; and there is a confession I must now make concerning the lecture Tom gave to that august body that night.

Tom was lecturing about a series of new routes he had made, climbing with Joe Brown and others in the Chamonix area – on the Aiguille Sans

Nom, the Leschaux and the Plan. He had no pictures to speak of from these climbs, so he looked around for transparencies amongst his friends' collections which looked something like the routes they had climbed. That evening the shots he showed of the *Great Diedre* on the Plan were actually mine, taken on the grooves and corners of the North Ridge of the Peigne, only projected the wrong way round. None of the pundits present recognised the difference.

In February 1966 Tom and I were joint guests at a Pinnacle Club Dinner, held on a Saturday evening in the Pen-y-Gwryd Hotel. This is the all ladies climbing club, and we had a wonderful time on this occasion with the girls of the Pinafore Club, as we used to call them. After the dinner we had a ceilidh and then, in the early hours, retreated with our hosts to stay in Cwm Dyli. This is the Pinnacle Club hut, situated on the flanks of Snowdon down the old Beddgelert road below the power station. At that date the hut was strictly for use by women only, but we were assured by the President, Countess Dorothea Gravina, that on this occasion an exception could be made.

Tom and I arrived at the carpark above the hut ahead of the Countess, and walked down the hill to its front door. There was a light inside and obviously some people were already in occupation. We opened the door and strode boldly inside, an action which caused something akin to an earthquake from the ladies inside the room. One burly female, smoking a clay pipe, rounded on us and met us at the door. "Get out! Get out! No men are allowed in here!" And we were physically bundled out by arms more powerful than ours, to watch the door slammed in our faces, without a chance to explain our presence. We met Dorothea on the track as we retreated, but, despite her offer to intercede with the ladies, neither Tom nor I dared brave the clay pipe smoker's wrath again, so fearsome had she appeared. Instead we spent what was left of the night sitting in the Skoda, talking until daylight dawned. Patey was a most interesting conversationalist, both humorous and understanding. With dawn came flutterings of snow, and the Doctor decided that this signified that conditions would be good on Lochnagar; he started up the engine and pointed the Skoda back north.

My most memorable trip with Tom was a visit to Applecross in March, 1966. We stayed in the hotel near the Bealach na Ba pass, where Tom had once been based while working as a locum for the local doctor. When we arrived, old friendships were renewed, and that evening, after a fine meal and a few drams, the music began to flow. We had a marvellous evening, singing and playing the accordion and banjo along with the locals playing an assortment of instruments. A heartening feature of these outposts in the

Highlands (the same is true in the West of Ireland) is that the people still know how to make their own music and enjoyment. They do not need that state of vicarious living which is now so prevalent in the conurbations of this country, where a few do and the rest are entertained by them.

The next day we solo-climbed several routes, including the famous *Cioch Nose* of Sgurr a'Chaorachain – a tremendous route – but as the daylight was ebbing (and with Tom a good day always finished in the dark) we were still scrambling, unroped, up the first long pitch of a climb Patey had pioneered solo in 1961, *The Sword of Gideon*. It lies on a buttress a few minutes up from the Bealach na Ba road, on the north side of the pass; its start is reached in a few minutes by scrambling up easy ledges.

"Have we still time to do this climb?" I ventured, pausing on a large step as we climbed the first pitch, by now worried about the lateness of the hour.

"Och aye, once you're up to that steep middle section up there, it's hard for a wee while, then after that it's only scrambling," Tom assured me. This turned out to be the understatement of the decade. We scrambled up on large holds, first traversing over to the left, then directly up and then right, until we reached the base of the vertical section of the buttress.

"Christ, Tom, it looks hard to solo!" I noted as I stood on a large glacis, looking up the wall above me in the gathering gloom. We had already climbed 150 feet of steep rock, possibly about Very Difficult in standard, and I was beginning to get gripped about the prospect of attempting the wall above without any protection.

"I did climb it solo when I first climbed it, you know!" Tom noted. "It's nae sae bad, barely VS, but if you prefer, we can put the rope on!" I looked again up the wall above me. There seemed dozens of feet of steep rock, beginning with a holdless groove, and the sandstone was so compact that it looked as if there would be little in the way of protection.

"I'll go first, if you like!" Patey decided, and before I could comment further he set off up the groove. I followed on just behind him, all too aware that the situation was compounded by climbing in boots, with lightweight rucksacks on our backs. I was immediately in difficulties and, after about ten feet, thought about retreating, but was then lured on by what seemed a jug out on my left. It turned out not to be one, but by then I was committed. Tom was doing his thing above me, his knees being used to good effect, and somehow he was moving upwards, despite his apparent flouting of what is a secure and sound technique. Soon he was a long way above me, and I was stuck in the groove. Then I saw him moving left, and he disappeared from view.

Trevor Jones on the difficult pitch of the *Sword of Gideon*, Applecross.   Photo: W Birkett

I had either to retreat or follow him. I could not do the former – a couple of vain attempts soon convinced me of this – but with a long reach I managed to get moving upwards again. I had to admit that it seemed as well to solo the route as lead it, for there was little or no protection in the groove; but when I had plucked up the courage and climbed this, the prospect that faced me from there on made my heart sink. Tom was out of sight, but I could hear him grunting and, in response to my anxious shouts through the darkness, I heard him calling, "Traverse left." I tried, but could not.

"I can't do it!" I croaked. "Step down and try that way," he responded from somewhere above. I did this and managed to start climbing leftwards, and then found I was on the crux of the climb so far. It is in fact the hardest move of the climb.

"Tom, Tom, I need a rope!"

"Yae what?" came down a voice, obviously also personally engrossed with survival. "I want a top rope!" But nothing happened, despite my waiting, and so I gritted my teeth and made a two-step move above two hundred feet of space, knowing a fall would be fatal. I began to shake and was croaking, "Tom, Tom, Tom," as I moved along, but somehow I managed to get across the traverse and then, almost immediately, the standard of the climb eased, and I could see Tom above me in a gloomy recess, a cigarette glowing in the dark. He was wedged securely into a fissure and, as I climbed up to him, he chuckled, "We can rope up here, if you want, but we really ought to be getting on up the crag. The rest is nae sae bad. I'll solo up, and if it gets hard, I'll throw you an end down."

Immediately above the recess was a crack, and starting this seemed hard. Tom played around for a while before making a strenuous pull, after which he climbed quickly up to a roof and then traversed to the right, disappearing once more from view. It was so dark now that I took off my rucksack and got out my head-torch. I put it on over my balaclava and, by its light, set forth. I managed the first pull off the ledge, and then realised in a panic that I had to keep climbing, for I could not rest until I reached the roof and the start of the traverse. Once I was up to that point I found with relief that I could stop to take a breather. I then managed to move right to reach a corner, but by now it was totally dark and, despite my head-torch, I just could not see well enough to climb.

"Tom, Tom, I'm stuck..." No response. Then there was a movement in the dark above me and there, framed on the edge of the corner by the light of my head-torch, was Patey.

"It's full of good holds, mon, once you move up," he assured me.

"Are you certain?" I begged, remembering the climbing below. "You said that about the first groove."

"Well, it's a long time since I made this climb," he defended himself.

"Oh hell!" I thought. "Here goes." I pulled up and made a sort of weird straddle move; and there, just as Tom had said, was a good hold, and then another and then another. And soon I was with him, laughing at my weakness.

"That was desperate," I gasped, once I had recovered and was sitting beside him on a ledge.

"Just a wee Scottish VS. In the Cairngorms it might just be graded Severe!" he assured me.

"The North-West is like Yorkshire," I opined, "VS means anything from desperate to impossible. But how do we go from here?"

"It's easy," he said. "Follow me," and, despite the fact that he had no head-torch, I could not keep pace with him as we scrambled up the last pitch. Fortunately, the climbing was easy, and even in the dark it turned out to be not such a bad proposition for, despite its steepness, it was only about Difficult in standard.

Ten minutes later we were on the top of the buttress and, looking at my watch, I realised we had climbed the 350-foot route in 40 minutes. The descent was to be something else, however, when my head-torch failed. An hour later found us swinging through the air on the end of Tom's old 'for emergencies only' rope. And it was almost another hour before we reached the safety of the road, the Skoda and the bar of the Hotel. Why it should have taken so long I cannot now say, for the present-day guide-book assures one that on the descent a traverse left to reach easy ground allows a swift retreat to the road in a matter of minutes. It also grades the climb Hard Very Severe and the middle pitch 5A. Perhaps our difficulties came about because we mistakenly descended on the steep right-hand side of the buttress. That evening, back at the hotel, it was a case of eat, drink, be merry and sing – to celebrate a truly memorable day.

Climbing with Tom was always an adventure. That was the spirit with which he entered into any enterprise, and it is a credo that makes for enjoyment and satisfaction as a mountaineer. His death from a freak abseiling accident while descending a sea-stack, The Maiden, in May, 1970 was one of the most tragic losses during the long period I have been climbing. It is hard to convey, to those who never knew him, his friends' great sense of loss; but some indication can be understood from the remark Joe Brown (not given to verbose overstatement): "It was worth driving all the way up to the Highlands just to climb and socialise with Tom." For, as Patey himself once wrote, "The Cairngorms climbing fraternity has always been a closely-knit community, linked by similar ideals and aspirations. Good climbing and good company often go together; each is essential to the enjoyment of the other. In the Cairngorms they are inseparable." I wish to finish by echoing those thoughts, which apply equally to Tom himself.